# THE ULTIMATE

**ROBERT KINZEL**

# NINJA SPEEDI

## COOKBOOK FOR BEGINNERS

*Effortless and Delicious Recipes for Family and Busy People on a Budget, Rapid Cooker and Air Fryer Cookbook*

# TABLE OF

# CONTENT

## CHAPTER 4 FISH AND SEAFOOD    *27*

## CHAPTER 5 VEGETABLES    *36*

# INTRODUCTION

Are you tired of spending hours in the kitchen trying to get a meal on the table for your family? Eating out can get quite expensive, but you also are limited on the amount of time and energy that you have to complete a meal on some evenings as well. Finding a way to get meals on the table and feed that hungry family can sometimes be a challenge.

The Ninja Speedi Rapid Cooker could be the solution that you are looking for. This is one of the newest additions that you will find to the revolutionary Ninja multi-cooker line. Similar to some of the other cookers in this family of products, you will find so much to love about the Ninja Speedi for your cooking needs.

Let's dive right in and learn more about the Ninja Speedi Rapid Cooker and why it is one appliance that you need to add to your kitchen today.

# CHAPTER 1 THE NINJA SPEEDI RAPID COOKER & AIR FRYER BASICS

The Ninja Speedi Rapid Cooker & Air Fryer is a great addition to any kitchen. To start, you will find that this model of cooker will come with 12 cooking functions, helping you to cook a wide variety of meals, much faster than you can do with some of the other kitchen appliances in your home. From air frying, steaming, baking, and rapid cooking, you will have dinner on the table in no time at all.

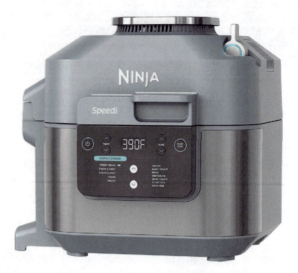

Another great feature of this cooker is that you can use all of the different cooking functions, without having to search around to find a new lid. Some of the older Ninja cookers required that you swap out lids based on the cooking method you chose to use. This is no longer a problem with the Ninja Speedi. With just one lid, you can cook on all the settings.

The newest feature that most customers will like is the rapid cooking system. Instead of the pressure cooking feature that is found on most other Ninja products, this model is going to introduce us to something known as the Rapid Cooking Technology. What makes this unique compared to some of the other functions on Ninja products?

This function is unique in that it will allow you to cook any one-pot meal that you would like in 15 minutes or less. This is definitely where the name of Speedi comes into play. You will also enjoy some of the other cooking functions that can make dinner time a little bit easier. You will be amazed at some of the different meals that you can make in 15 minutes or less when you use this device and we will take a look at some of the different options here.

The Ninja Speedi comes with a 6-qt capacity pot to help you make your meals. This is enough to feed a family of four and probably have some leftovers as well, making it a great option for your family. This is enough to have one pound of pasta and 4 chicken breasts at the same time inside.

## RAPID COOKING AND SMARTSWITCH FUNCTION

Two of the functions that you will be able to enjoy with the Ninja Speedi appliance are the Rapid Coking System and the SmartSwitch Functionality.

To start is the rapid cooking system. This feature is going to allow the user a way to create moisture with the help of steam while also caramelizing and crisping with the use of the air fryer function all in one pot. This can speed up the process of cooking because you can cook tender vegetables, fluffy rice, and the juiciest of chicken all in the same pot at the same time, without having to use a lot of different parts in the kitchen or waiting to do each one.

There is also the SmartSwitch functionality. This one can be nice to use because it allows you to switch between the Rapid Cooker and the Air Fry mode whenever you would like, opening up a lot of possibilities when you are cooking your meals. You can cook some of your favorites that are usually reserved for the air fryer, such as chicken wings and fries, or you can switch it around to get the whole meal cooked in about 15 minutes too.

### Do I Need to Prepare Foods Before Putting Into Ninja Speedi?

The next thing to consider is how much time you will need to spend preparing the food before you place it into the Ninja Speedi. This is one of the other great features that you are going to enjoy about this appliance. Many foods will not need any preparation at all. It is even possible to take some frozen foods and add them into the appliance, getting it cooked up in no time.

There are some recipes that will ask for a bit of preparation of the food before you put them into the appliance. This will depend on what you are cooking and how involved you would like to be. But there are still many recipes that allow you to throw the ingredients into the Ninja Speedi, push a few buttons and you are ready to go.

### Can the Ninja Speedi Really Air Fry, Steam and Broil?

There are a lot of great things that the Ninja Speedi is able to do for you. This is one of the best air fryers out there to help you get the crispy fries and chicken nuggets that you would like when using the device. In fact. You do not need to put in a whole bunch of oil to get the taste as well. But what else would you expect from a great product from the Ninja line?

But it is some of the other features that come with the Ninja Speedi that make it stand out among the crowd. Not only will it make some great air fried foods, you will notice that it is really good at broiling and steaming as well. It is difficult to find a steaming function that can take those vegetables and make them perfect in just a matter of minutes. You can also use it to broil foods, including broiling your chicken to be golden brown, without overcooking it, in just 15 minutes for your whole family.

### Cook More Than One Food at a Time

One of the things that can make dinner take forever in the kitchen is that you will need to cook each food on its own to make sure that it turns out perfectly. You do not want to cook the vegetables and the chicken and the rice at the same time because they need different cooking methods. This can cause a big mess and make the process take twice as long as before.

When you use the simple Speedi Meals setting and some of the guidelines put in with your appliance, you will be able to cook vegetables, protein, and a starch all at the same time and often in half an hour or less. And they will all come out perfectly, giving you the great tastes that you are looking for with each meal.

**It is Easy to Use**

When you hear all of these great benefits, you may assume that the Ninja Speedi is going to be difficult for you to use. This can make some consumers worry about purchasing this item and whether it is going to be a good option for you. Despite all of the different functions that come with the Ninja Speedi, you will find that it is a really easy option to use.

You simply start with a lever that will help you to switch between the Rapid Cooker and the Air Fryer. This is really easy for you to flip around. Once that is done, you will just need to pick the cooking program, the temperature, and the amount of time the meal needs to cook. These will often be provided in the recipe that you choose and there are some default times and temperatures that are suggested based on the setting you choose, but these are easy to change as well.

In addition, there is no automatic preheat cycle, but the manual does recommend that you add about 5 minutes to the cooking times on air frying and bake & roast to help heat up the cooker before you start cooking to make sure it is warm enough for your needs. Overall, this is one of the easiest products to use on the market and can give you some amazing results.

## THE BENEFITS OF THE NINJA SPEEDI RAPID COOKER

For those who are already fans of the Ninja Cooker, you will find that there is even more to love when you choose the Ninja Speedi Rapid Cooker. There are a ton of benefits that you are able to enjoy with this kitchen appliance and you may find that you use it more than any other appliance in the kitchen once you bring it home.

There are a number of benefits that you can enjoy with the Ninja Speedi Rapid Cooker and some of them include:
- Excellent design that can get food cooked fast.
- 12 cooking functions between the two modes to make cooking easier.
- Cooking functions that you are able to customize the way that you want.

- One smart lid so you won't have to worry about swapping the lids to get the meal done.
- Rapid cooking technology to speed things up a bit in the kitchen.
- Easy SmartSwitch Functionality
- The ability to crisp and steam the food at the same time
- Rectangular design to safe space in the cupboard
- Safe to clean in the dishwasher to save time
- Nonstick-coated cooking pot
- 1-year warranty
- Touch-screen display so you are in control over the food

While there are a number of things to love about the Ninja Speedi, you will find that there are a few drawbacks to choosing this over another option. One issue is that you can only purchase it in the 6-quart capacity. If you would like one that is smaller or bigger, this can be a problem. This appliance is also quite bulky, taking up a lot of space on the countertop if you choose to leave it there. You may need to free up some cupboard space to put it away when not in use.

## THE MODES OF THE NINJA SPEEDI RAPID COOKER

Now it is time for us to take a look at some of the ways that you can cook with the Ninja Speedi Rapid Coker. There are two modes of cooking that you are able to find when you choose to work with this cooker. The two main cooking options include:

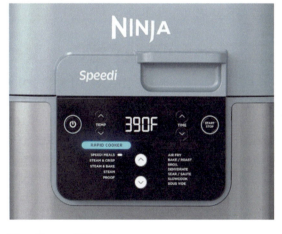

### Rapid Cooker Mode

The first mode is the Rapid Cooker mode. This is going to work exactly like you do with a combi oven. A combi oven is able to do three different techniques for cooking all in the same appliance, including steam, convection, and a combination of the two.

Convection is the one that you will want to use when baking and the steam function is best when you would like to directly cook the food items in the oven. You can even combine the two methods to make sure that you get juicier and more flavorful meals. Combination cooking is also great when you want to preserve the nutrients and the moisture in the food as well.

The Rapid Cooker Mode is going to use some of the same technology that you can find in the combi oven. You can choose to do a few functions under this including:

- Speedi Meals
- Steam & Crisp
- Steam & Bake
- Steam
- Proof

The idea here is that you will see steam generated from the bottom while using convection heat from the top. You will be able to make almost all types of food including vegetables and meat utilizing this function. If there is a type of food that often dries out in the air fryer, then you can choose the Rapid Cooker mode to help with that.

**Air Fryer Mode**

The second mode that you can use for the Ninja Speedi Rapid Cooker is the Air Fryer mode. This one is going to be a multi-cooker option that will come with a number of functions that you are able to use. Some of these functions include:

- Air Fry
- Bake/Roast
- Air Broil
- Dehydrate
- Sear/Sauté
- Slow Cook
- Sous Vide

The Air Fryer mode is going to use convection heat to help you get the food cooked efficiently, while also provide a crispier finish. You will love that the veggies, fish, and crispy meat with little to no oil at all. This makes the food healthier and cheaper, while still making it feel like you are cheating a little bit as well. You can use this mode for many types of food, but it seems to be effective when you would like to prepare some of the best frozen foods too.

## ACCESSORIES FOR THE NINJA SPEEDI RAPID COOKER

If you have used the Ninja Cooker in the past, you may be surprised that the Ninja Speedi is not going to come with a ton of extra accessories. When you purchase this version, you will get a 6-quart cooking pot and a crisper plate. That is it.

However, you will quickly notice that the crisper plate that comes with it is pretty unique. While you are air frying, you can place the crisper plate right at the bottom of the cooking pot. When you are trying to do some rapid cooking, you can use the crisper plate like an elevated position, similar to a rack, and make more than one meal at the same time.

Both the crisper plate and the cooking pot are also nonstick coated so that your food will not stick to the bottom. They are also safe to place in the dishwasher, making cleanup of your Ninja Speedi a little easier.

## CLEANING HE NINJA SPEEDI RAPID COOKER

When you are done with your Ninja Speedi, you need to take the time to clean the whole product. If you leave food in it and do not do a good scrub of the machine, you could end up with a big mess to handle.

To start, the accessories that come with the Ninja Speedi are going to be safe to place into the dishwasher. You can just pop them right in and not worry about having to scrub and clean those by hand. You should not put the Ninja Speedi into the dishwasher, but manually cleaning it is simple.

To clean, you need to manually rinse off any leftover food residue form the cooking pat and its crisper plate. If some of the food is really stuck in the cooker, then you can soak them For the main unit, you will want to wipe it clean using a damp cloth. Wipe clean again with a dry dish towel to help make sure that food is not left behind and the Ninja Speedi will be able to keep the right glossiness.

There are a ton of great options out there to help you make some delicious snacks and meals with the Ninja Speedi. Now that you know a little bit more about it, you can dive right in and make the meals of your dreams.

## CONCLUSION

There are so many reasons why you should love the Ninja Speedi Rapid Cooker & Air Fryer. It has a lot of great functions that can make cooking a breeze and can ensure that you will be able to get supper on the table for your family in no time at all. Some recipes can even be done in 15 minutes! This can make life so much easier than bringing out all those pots and pans and hoping that things are going to work for a big dinner.

If you have never used one of the Ninja Foodi products in the past, you may take a look at some of these recipes and assume that they are going to be difficult to work with or that it is impossible to work with the different types of food in one pot. But one great meal into using this device, and you will see exactly why this is worth the purchase. Before long, you will be looking through this cookbook to figure out how many meals you can make with the Ninja Speedi in a week.

We are now going to take a closer look at some of the amazing recipes that you are able to make when you use the Ninja Speedi. This will ensure that you are able to get all the great tastes and see what this device is able to do in the first place. Some of the recipes in this guidebook will be simple to make, and some will bring in the full potential that comes with the Ninja Speedi as well. And of course, we are going to add in some of your classic favorites that you just can't miss out on when using this appliance in your home.

So, let's dive in and see more about what the Ninja Speedi Rapid Cooker is able to do for your cooking needs.

# BASIC KITCHEN CONVERSIONS & EQUIVALENTS

## DRY MEASUREMENTS CONVERSION CHART

3 teaspoons = 1 tablespoon = 1/16 cup

6 teaspoons = 2 tablespoons = 1/8 cup

12 teaspoons = 4 tablespoons = ¼ cup

24 teaspoons = 8 tablespoons = ½ cup

36 teaspoons = 12 tablespoons = ¾ cup

48 teaspoons = 16 tablespoons = 1 cup

## METRIC TO US COOKING CONVERSIONS

## OVEN TEMPERATURES

120 ºC = 250 ºF

160 ºC = 320 ºF

180 ºC = 350 ºF

205 ºC = 400 ºF

220 ºC = 425 ºF

## LIQUID MEASUREMENTS

## CONVERSION CHART

8 fluid ounces = 1 cup = ½ pint = ¼ quart

16 fluid ounces = 2 cups = 1 pint = ½ quart

32 fluid ounces = 4 cups = 2 pints = 1 quart = ¼ gallon

128 fluid ounces = 16 cups = 8 pints = 4

quarts = 1 gallon

## BAKING IN GRAMS

1 cup flour = 140 grams

1 cup sugar = 150 grams

1 cup powdered sugar = 160 grams

1 cup heavy cream = 235 grams

## VOLUME

1 milliliter = 1/5 teaspoon

5 ml = 1 teaspoon

15 ml = 1 tablespoon

240 ml = 1 cup or 8 fluid ounces

1 liter = 34 fluid ounces

## WEIGHT

1 gram = .035 ounces

100 grams = 3.5 ounces

500 grams = 1.1 pounds

1 kilogram = 35 ounces

## US TO METRIC COOKING CONVERSIONS

1/5 tsp = 1 ml

1 tsp = 5 ml

1 tbsp = 15 ml

1 fluid ounces = 30 ml

1 cup = 237 ml

1 pint (2 cups) = 473 ml

1 quart (4 cups) = .95 liter

1 gallon (16 cups) = 3.8 liters

1 oz = 28 grams

1 pound = 454 grams

## BUTTER

1 cup butter = 2 sticks = 8 ounces = 230 grams = 16 tablespoons

## WHAT DOES 1 CUP EQUAL

1 cup = 8 fluid ounces

1 cup = 16 tablespoons

1 cup = 48 teaspoons

1 cup = ½ pint

1 cup = ¼ quart

1 cup = 1/16 gallon

1 cup = 240 ml

## BAKING PAN CONVERSIONS

9-inch round cake pan = 12 cups

10-inch tube pan =16 cups

10-inch bundt pan = 12 cups

9-inch springform pan = 10 cups

9 x 5 inch loaf pan = 8 cups

9-inch square pan = 8 cups

## BAKING PAN CONVERSIONS

1 cup all-purpose flour = 4.5 oz

1 cup rolled oats = 3 oz

1 large egg = 1.7 oz

1 cup butter = 8 oz

1 cup milk = 8 oz

1 cup heavy cream = 8.4 oz

1 cup granulated sugar = 7.1 oz

1 cup packed brown sugar = 7.75 oz

1 cup vegetable oil = 7.7 oz

1 cup unsifted powdered sugar = 4.4 oz

# CHAPTER 2
# BREAKFAST

## CINNAMON NUTTY BAKED APPLES (SLOW COOK)

Prep Time: 15 minutes, Cook Time: 5 hours, Serves: 8

### INGREDIENTS:

- 8 large apples
- 1½ cups buckwheat flakes
- 1 cup chopped walnuts
- ½ cup apple juice
- ⅓ cup coconut sugar
- 6 tbsps. unsalted butter, cut into pieces
- 2 tbsps. freshly squeezed lemon juice
- 1 tsp. ground cinnamon
- ¼ tsp. salt

### DIRECTIONS:

1. Before getting started, be sure to remove the crisper tray.
2. Peel a strip of skin around the top of each apple to prevent splitting. Gently remove the apple core, making sure not to cut all the way through to the bottom. Coat the apples with lemon juice and keep aside.
3. Mix the buckwheat flakes, walnuts, coconut sugar, cinnamon, and salt in a medium bowl.
4. Pour the melted butter over the buckwheat mixture and mix until crumbly. Stuff the apples with this mixture, rounding the stuffing on top of each apple.
5. Arrange the stuffed apples in the bottom of the pot. Add the apple juice around the apples.
6. Close the lid and flip the SmartSwitch to AIRFRY/STOVETOP. Select SLOW COOK, set temperature to "Lo", and set time to 5 hours. Press START/STOP to begin cooking, until the apples are very soft.
7. Enjoy!

## FRENCH TOAST STICKS (BAKE&ROAST)

Prep Time: 10 minutes, Cook Time: 5 minutes, Serves: 4

### INGREDIENTS:

- cooking spray
- 4 bread, sliced into sticks
- 2 tbsps. soft butter or margarine
- 2 eggs, gently beaten
- Salt, to taste
- 1 pinch cinnamon
- 1 pinch nutmeg
- 1 pinch ground cloves

### DIRECTIONS:

1. Push in the legs on the Crisper Tray, then place the tray in the bottom of the pot. Spray a 8-inch round baking pan with cooking spray.
2. Whisk eggs with salt, cinnamon, nutmeg and ground cloves in a bowl.
3. Dip the bread sticks in the egg mixture and place in the baking pan.
4. Close the lid and flip the SmartSwitch to AIRFRY/STOVETOP. Select BAKE & ROAST, set temperature to 375°F, and set time to 10 minutes (unit will need to preheat for 5 minutes, so set an external timer if desired). Press START/STOP to begin cooking.
5. When the unit is preheated and the time reaches 5 minutes, place the pan on the tray. Close the lid to begin cooking, flipping in between.
6. Dish out and serve warm.

## SWEET POTATO HASH (STEAM&CRISP)

Prep: 10 minutes, Total Cook Time: 17 minutes, Steam: approx. 4 minutes, Cook: 13 minutes, Serves: 6

### INGREDIENTS:

- ½ cup water, for steaming
- 2 large sweet potato, cut into small cubes
- 2 slices bacon, cut into small pieces
- 2 tbsps. olive oil
- 1 tbsp. smoked paprika
- 1 tsp. sea salt
- 1 tsp. ground black pepper
- 1 tsp. dried dill weed

### DIRECTIONS:

1. Pour ½ cup water into the pot. Push in the legs on the Crisper Tray, then place the tray in the bottom position in the pot.
2. Mix together sweet potato, bacon, olive oil, paprika, salt, black pepper and dill in a large bowl.
3. Transfer the mixture on the tray.
4. Close the lid and flip the SmartSwitch to Rapid Cooker. Select STEAM & CRISP, set temperature to 390°F, and set time to 13 minutes. Press START/STOP to begin cooking (the unit will steam for approx. 4 minutes before crisping).
5. With 5 minutes remaining, open the lid and toss the mixture with tongs. Close the lid to continue cooking.
6. Dish out and serve warm.

## PEANUT BUTTER BANANA BREAD (STEAM&BAKE)

Prep: 15 minutes, Total Cook Time: 45 minutes, Steam: approx. 25 minutes, Cook: 20 minutes, Serves: 6

### INGREDIENTS:

- 3 cups water, for steaming
- cooking spray
- 1 cup plus 1 tbsp. all-purpose flour
- 1¼ tsps. baking powder
- 1 large egg
- 2 medium ripe bananas, peeled and mashed
- ¾ cup walnuts, roughly chopped
- ¼ tsp. salt
- ⅓ cup granulated sugar
- ¼ cup canola oil
- 2 tbsps. creamy peanut butter
- 2 tbsps. sour cream
- 1 tsp. vanilla extract

### DIRECTIONS:

1. Pour 3 cups water into the pot. Push in the legs on the Crisper Tray, then place the tray in the bottom position in the pot. Spray a 8-inch round baking pan with cooking spray.
2. Mix together the flour, baking powder and salt in a bowl.
3. Whisk together egg with sugar, canola oil, sour cream, peanut butter and vanilla extract in a bowl.
4. Stir in the bananas and beat until well combined.
5. Now, add the flour mixture and fold in the walnuts gently.
6. Mix until combined and transfer the mixture evenly into the prepared baking pan, then place the pan on the tray.
7. Close the lid and flip the SmartSwitch to Rapid Cooker. Select STEAM & BAKE, set temperature to 350°F, and set time to 20 minutes. Press START/STOP to begin cooking (the unit will steam for approx. 25 minutes before baking).
8. When cooking is complete, carefully remove the pan and place onto a wire rack to cool.
9. Cut the bread into desired size slices and serve.

## CREAMY PARSLEY SOUFFLÉ (STEAM&BAKE)

Prep: 5 minutes, Total Cook Time: 30 minutes, Steam: approx. 20 minutes, Cook: 10 minutes, Serves: 2

### INGREDIENTS:

- 1 cup water, for steaming
- cooking spray
- 2 eggs
- 1 tbsp. fresh parsley, chopped
- 1 fresh red chili pepper, chopped
- 2 tbsps. light cream
- Salt, to taste

### DIRECTIONS:

1. Pour 1 cup water into the pot. Push in the legs on the Crisper Tray, then place the tray in the bottom position in the pot. Spray 2 soufflé dishes with cooking spray.
2. Mix together all the ingredients in a bowl until well combined.
3. Transfer the mixture into prepared soufflé dishes and place on the tray.
4. Close the lid and flip the SmartSwitch to Rapid Cooker. Select STEAM & BAKE, set temperature to 350°F, and set time to 10 minutes. Press START/STOP to begin cooking (the unit will steam for approx. 20 minutes before baking).
5. When cooking is complete, dish out to serve warm.

## BREAKFAST FRITTATA (STEAM&BAKE)

Prep: 15 minutes, Total Cook Time: 32 minutes, Steam: approx. 20 minutes, Cook: 12 minutes, Serves: 2

### INGREDIENTS:

- 1 cup water, for steaming
- cooking spray
- ¼ pound breakfast sausage, fully cooked and crumbled
- 4 eggs, lightly beaten
- ½ cup Monterey Jack cheese, shredded
- 2 tbsps. red bell pepper, diced
- 1 green onion, chopped
- 1 pinch cayenne pepper

### DIRECTIONS:

1. Pour 1 cup water into the pot. Push in the legs on the Crisper Tray, then place the tray in the bottom position in the pot. Spray a 8-inch round baking pan with cooking spray.
2. Whisk together eggs with sausage, green onion, bell pepper, cheese and cayenne in a bowl.
3. Transfer the egg mixture in the prepared baking pan and place on the tray.
4. Close the lid and flip the SmartSwitch to Rapid Cooker. Select STEAM & BAKE, set temperature to 350°F, and set time to 12 minutes. Press START/STOP to begin cooking (the unit will steam for approx. 20 minutes before baking).
5. Serve warm.

## BREAKFAST ZUCCHINI (STEAM&CRISP)

Prep: 5 minutes, Total Cook Time: 24 minutes, Steam: approx. 4 minutes, Cook: 20 minutes, Serves: 4

### INGREDIENTS:

- ½ cup water, for steaming
- 4 zucchinis, diced into 1-inch pieces, drained
- 2 small bell pepper, chopped medium
- 2 small onion, chopped medium
- Cooking oil spray
- Pinch salt and black pepper

### DIRECTIONS:

1. Pour ½ cup water into the pot. Push in the legs on the Crisper Tray, then place the tray in the bottom position in the pot. Spray the tray with cooking spray.
2. Season the zucchini with salt and black pepper and place on the tray.
3. Close the lid and flip the SmartSwitch to Rapid Cooker. Select STEAM & CRISP, set temperature to 350°F, and set time to 20 minutes. Press START/STOP to begin cooking (the unit will steam for approx. 4 minutes before crisping).
4. After 10 minutes, open the lid and stir the zucchini with tongs. Close the lid to continue cooking.
5. With 5 minutes remaining, open the lid. Add onion and bell pepper. Close the lid to continue cooking.
6. When cooking is complete, transfer into a serving plate. Mix well to serve warm.

## MUSHROOM AND TOMATO FRITTATA (STEAM&BAKE)

Prep: 15 minutes, Total Cook Time: 24 minutes, Steam: approx. 10 minutes, Cook: 14 minutes, Serves: 2

### INGREDIENTS:

- 1 cup water, for steaming
- cooking spray
- 1 bacon slice, chopped
- 6 cherry tomatoes, halved
- 6 fresh mushrooms, sliced
- 3 eggs
- ½ cup Parmesan cheese, grated
- 1 tbsp. olive oil
- Salt and black pepper, to taste

### DIRECTIONS:

1. Pour 1 cup water into the pot. Push in the legs on the Crisper Tray, then place the tray in the bottom position in the pot. Spray a 8-inch round baking pan with cooking spray.
2. Heat olive oil in a skillet over medium heat, add bacon, mushrooms, tomatoes, salt and black pepper. Sauté for 6 minutes. Transfer the bacon mixture to the baking pan.
3. Whisk together eggs in a small bowl and add cheese. Mix well and pour over the bacon mixture.
4. Place the baking pan on the tray.
5. Close the lid and flip the SmartSwitch to Rapid Cooker. Select STEAM & BAKE, set temperature to 350°F, and set time to 8 minutes. Press START/STOP to begin cooking (the unit will steam for approx. 10 minutes before baking).
6. When cooking is complete, dish out and serve hot.

## STYLISH HAM OMELET (STEAM&BAKE)

Prep: 10 minutes, Total Cook Time: 37 minutes, Steam: approx. 15 minutes, Cook: 22 minutes, Serves: 2

### INGREDIENTS:

- 1 cup water, for steaming
- cooking spray
- 4 small tomatoes, chopped
- 4 eggs
- 2 ham slices
- 1 onion, chopped
- 2 tbsps. cheddar cheese
- Salt and black pepper, to taste

### DIRECTIONS:

1. Pour 1 cup water into the pot. Push in the legs on the Crisper Tray, then place the tray in the bottom position in the pot. Spray a 8-inch round baking pan with cooking spray.
2. Heat a nonstick skillet on medium heat and add onion and ham. Stir fry for about 5 minutes.
3. Place the tomatoes in the baking pan, then transfer the pan on the tray.
4. Close the lid and flip the SmartSwitch to Rapid Cooker. Select STEAM & BAKE, set temperature to 350°F, and set time to 17 minutes. Press START/STOP to begin cooking (the unit will steam for approx. 15 minutes before baking).
5. With 10 minutes remaining, open the lid. Transfer the onion mixture into the pan. Whisk together eggs, cheddar cheese, salt and black pepper in a bowl and pour in the pan. Close the lid to continue cooking.
6. Dish out and serve warm.

## HEALTHY TOFU OMELET (STEAM&BAKE)

Prep: 10 minutes, Total Cook Time: 40 minutes, Steam: approx. 20 minutes, Cook: 20 minutes, Serves: 2

### INGREDIENTS:

- 1 cup water, for steaming
- cooking spray
- ¼ of onion, chopped
- 12-ounce silken tofu, pressed and sliced
- 3 eggs, beaten
- 1 tbsp. chives, chopped
- 1 garlic clove, minced
- 2 tsps. olive oil
- Salt and black pepper, to taste

### DIRECTIONS:

1. Pour 1 cup water into the pot. Push in the legs on the Crisper Tray, then place the tray in the bottom position in the pot. Spray a 8-inch round baking pan with cooking spray.
2. Add onion and garlic to the greased pan. Place the pan on the tray.
3. Close the lid and flip the SmartSwitch to Rapid Cooker. Select STEAM & BAKE, set temperature to 350°F, and set time to 20 minutes. Press START/STOP to begin cooking (the unit will steam for approx. 20 minutes before baking).
4. With 16 minutes remaining, open the lid. Add tofu, mushrooms and chives and season with salt and black pepper. Beat the eggs and pour over the tofu mixture. Close the lid to continue cooking, poking the eggs twice in between.
5. Dish out and serve warm.

## CHICKEN AND BROCCOLI QUICHE (STEAM&BAKE)

Prep: 15 minutes, Total Cook Time: 27 minutes, Steam: approx. 15 minutes, Cook: 12 minutes, Serves: 4

### INGREDIENTS:

- 1 cup water, for steaming
- 1 frozen ready-made pie crust
- 1 egg
- ⅓ cup cheddar cheese, grated
- ¼ cup boiled broccoli, chopped
- ¼ cup cooked chicken, chopped
- ½ tbsp. olive oil
- 3 tbsps. whipping cream
- Salt and black pepper, to taste

### DIRECTIONS:

1. Pour 1 cup water into the pot. Push in the legs on the Crisper Tray, then place the tray in the bottom position in the pot. Spray 2 small pie pans with cooking spray.
2. Whisk egg with whipping cream, cheese, salt and black pepper in a bowl.
3. Cut 2 (5-inch) rounds from the pie crust and arrange in each pie pan.
4. Press in the bottom and sides gently and pour the egg mixture over pie crust.
5. Top evenly with chicken and broccoli and place the pie pans on the tray.
6. Close the lid and flip the SmartSwitch to Rapid Cooker. Select STEAM & BAKE, set temperature to 390°F, and set time to 12 minutes. Press START/STOP to begin cooking (the unit will steam for approx. 15 minutes before baking).
7. Dish out to serve hot.

## EGGLESS SPINACH AND BACON QUICHE (STEAM&BAKE)

Prep: 15 minutes, Total Cook Time: 30 minutes, Steam: approx. 20 minutes, Cook: 10 minutes, Serves: 2

### INGREDIENTS:

- 1 cup water, for steaming
- cooking spray
- 1 cup fresh spinach, chopped
- 4 slices of bacon, cooked and chopped
- ½ cup mozzarella cheese, shredded
- 4 tbsps. milk
- 1 cup Parmesan cheese, shredded
- 4 dashes Tabasco sauce
- Salt and black pepper, to taste

### DIRECTIONS:

1. Pour 1 cup water into the pot. Push in the legs on the Crisper Tray, then place the tray in the bottom position in the pot. Spray a 8-inch round baking pan with cooking spray.
2. Mix together all the ingredients in a bowl and transfer the mixture into the prepared pan, then place the pan on the tray.
3. Close the lid and flip the SmartSwitch to Rapid Cooker. Select STEAM & BAKE, set temperature to 330°F, and set time to 10 minutes. Press START/STOP to begin cooking (the unit will steam for approx. 20 minutes before baking).
4. Dish out and serve warm.

## SPINACH AND EGG CUPS (STEAM&BAKE)

Prep: 15 minutes, Total Cook Time: 41 minutes, Steam: approx. 20 minutes, Cook: 21 minutes, Serves: 4

### INGREDIENTS:

- 1 cup water, for steaming
- 1 tbsp. unsalted butter, melted
- 1 pound fresh baby spinach
- 4 eggs
- 7 ounces ham, sliced
- 4 tsps. milk
- 1 tbsp. olive oil
- Salt and black pepper, to taste

### DIRECTIONS:

1. Pour 1 cup water into the pot. Push in the legs on the Crisper Tray, then place the tray in the bottom position in the pot. Grease 4 ramekins with butter.
2. Heat olive oil in a pan and add spinach.
3. Sauté for about 3 minutes and drain the liquid completely from the spinach.
4. Divide the spinach equally into the prepared ramekins and add ham slices.
5. Crack 1 egg over ham in each ramekin and pour milk evenly over eggs.
6. Season with salt and black pepper and transfer the ramekins on the tray.
7. Close the lid and flip the SmartSwitch to Rapid Cooker. Select STEAM & BAKE, set temperature to 350°F, and set time to 18 minutes. Press START/STOP to begin cooking (the unit will steam for approx. 20 minutes before baking).
8. Serve warm.

## SAUSAGE SOLO (STEAM&BAKE)

Prep: 5 minutes, Total Cook Time: 35 minutes, Steam: approx. 20 minutes, Cook: 15 minutes, Serves: 4

### INGREDIENTS:

- 1 cup water, for steaming
- cooking spray
- 6 eggs
- 4 cooked sausages, sliced
- 2 bread slices, cut into sticks
- ½ cup mozzarella cheese, grated
- ½ cup cream

### DIRECTIONS:

1. Pour 1 cup water into the pot. Push in the legs on the Crisper Tray, then place the tray in the bottom position in the pot. Spray 4 ramekins with cooking spray.
2. Whisk together eggs and cream in a bowl and beat well.
3. Transfer the egg mixture into ramekins and arrange the bread sticks and sausage slices around the edges.
4. Top with mozzarella cheese evenly and place the ramekins on the tray.
5. Close the lid and flip the SmartSwitch to Rapid Cooker. Select STEAM & BAKE, set temperature to 350°F, and set time to 15 minutes. Press START/STOP to begin cooking (the unit will steam for approx. 20 minutes before baking).
6. When cooking is complete, dish out to serve warm.


## SAUSAGE FRITTATA (STEAM&BAKE)

Prep: 15 minutes, Total Cook Time: 22 minutes, Steam: approx. 10 minutes, Cook: 12 minutes, Serves: 2

### INGREDIENTS:

- 1 cup water, for steaming
- cooking spray
- ½ of chorizo sausage, sliced
- ½ cup frozen corn
- 1 large potato, boiled, peeled and cubed
- 3 jumbo eggs
- 2 tbsps. feta cheese, crumbled
- 1 tbsp. olive oil
- Salt and black pepper, to taste

### DIRECTIONS:

1. Pour 1 cup water into the pot. Push in the legs on the Crisper Tray, then place the tray in the bottom position in the pot. Spray a 8-inch round baking pan with cooking spray.
2. Whisk together eggs with salt and black pepper in a bowl.
3. Heat olive oil in a skillet over medium heat, add sausage, corn and potato. Sauté for 5 minutes. Then transfer into the baking pan and stir in the whisked eggs. Place on the tray and top with cheese.
4. Close the lid and flip the SmartSwitch to Rapid Cooker. Select STEAM & BAKE, set temperature to 350°F, and set time to 7 minutes. Press START/STOP to begin cooking (the unit will steam for approx. 10 minutes before baking).
5. When cooking is complete, dish out and serve hot.

# CHAPTER 3
# POULTRY

## CILANTRO DIJON CHICKEN CUTLETS (SEAR/SAUTÉ)

Prep Time: 10 minutes, Cook Time: 12 minutes, Serves: 4

### INGREDIENTS:

- 4 boneless skinless chicken breast halves
- ¼ cup chopped fresh cilantro
- 1 tbsp. Dijon mustard
- 1 tbsp. butter
- ½ cup prepared salsa
- 2 tbsps. fresh lime juice

### DIRECTIONS:

1. Before getting started, be sure to remove the Crisper Tray from the pot.
2. Arrange each chicken breast between 2 plastic wrap sheets and with a meat mallet, pound into ½-inch thickness.
3. Spread mustard over each breast.
4. Flip the SmartSwitch to AIRFRY/STOVETOP. Select SEAR/SAUTÉ, choose "3". Press START/STOP to begin cooking.
5. Melt the butter in the pot and sauté the chicken for about 3 to 4 minutes per side.
6. Stir in the salsa and lime juice and simmer, uncovered for about 6 to 8 minutes.
7. Serve with a sprinkling of the cilantro.

## BROCCOLI CHICKEN (SEAR/SAUTÉ)

Prep Time: 15 minutes, Cook Time: 15 minutes, Serves: 4

### INGREDIENTS:

- 1 tbsp. Shaoxing rice wine
- 2 tsps. light soy sauce
- 1 tsp. minced garlic
- 1 tsp. cornstarch
- ¼ tsp. sugar
- ¾ pound (340 g) boneless, skinless chicken thighs, cut into 2-inch chunks
- 2 tbsps. vegetable oil
- 4 peeled fresh ginger slices, about the size of a quarter
- Kosher salt
- 1 pound (454 g) broccoli, cut into bite-size florets
- 2 tbsps. water
- Red pepper flakes (optional)
- ¼ cup store-bought black bean sauce

### DIRECTIONS:

1. Before getting started, be sure to remove the Crisper Tray from the pot.
2. In a small bowl, mix together the rice wine, light soy, garlic, cornstarch, and sugar. Add the chicken and marinate for 10 minutes.
3. Flip the SmartSwitch to AIRFRY/STOVETOP. Select SEAR/SAUTÉ, choose "4". Press START/STOP to begin cooking.
4. Pour in the vegetable oil in the pot. Add the ginger and a pinch of salt. Allow the ginger to sizzle for about 30 seconds, swirling gently.
5. Transfer the chicken to the pot, discarding the marinade. Sear the chicken for 4 to 5 minutes, until no longer pink. Add the broccoli, water, and a pinch of red pepper flakes (if using) and sear for 1 minute. Close the lid and cook the broccoli for 6 to 8 minutes, until it is crisp-tender.
6. Stir in the black bean sauce until coated and heated through, about 2 minutes, or until the sauce has thickened slightly and become glossy.
7. Discard the ginger, transfer to a platter, and serve hot.

## KERALA CURRY (SEAR/SAUTÉ)

Prep Time: 20 minutes, Cook Time: 50 minutes, Serves: 8

### INGREDIENTS:

- 1 (3-pound / 1.4-kg) chicken, cut into pieces
- 1 tsp. ground black pepper
- ¼ cup vegetable oil
- Salt to taste
- 2 onions, chopped
- 5 russet potatoes, peeled and cut into 1-inch pieces
- 8 cloves garlic, chopped
- ¼ cup mild curry powder
- 2 tbsps. hot curry powder

### DIRECTIONS:

1. Before getting started, be sure to remove the Crisper Tray from the pot.
2. Flip the SmartSwitch to AIRFRY/STOVETOP. Select SEAR/SAUTÉ, choose "4". Press START/STOP to begin cooking.
3. Add the chicken in the pot and enough water to cover and bring to a boil.
4. Reduce the heat from "4" to "3" and simmer for about 20 minutes.
5. Meanwhile in a large wok, heat the vegetable oil on medium heat and sauté the onion and garlic for about 5 minutes.
6. Stir in both curry powders, black pepper and salt and sauté for about 5 minutes.
7. Transfer the onion mixture into the pot with the chicken.
8. Stir in the potatoes and simmer for about 20 minutes.

## SESAME CHICKEN AND BEAN RICE (SPEEDI MEALS)

Prep: 20 minutes, Total Cook Time: 25 minutes, Steam: approx. 10 minutes, Cook: 15 minutes, Serves: 4

### INGREDIENTS:

- LEVEL 1 (BOTTOM OF POT)
- 1 cup white rice, rinsed
- 1 cup canned black beans, drained
- 2 cups water
- LEVEL 2 (TRAY)
- 1½ cups soy sauce
- 2 tsps. chicken seasoning
- 1½ lbs. chicken breasts or thighs
- TOPPING:
- 2 tbsps. toasted sesame seeds

### DIRECTIONS:

1. Place all Level 1 ingredients in the pot and stir to combine.
2. Pull out the legs on the Crisper Tray, then place the tray in the elevated position in the pot.
3. In a large bowl, mix the chicken with soy sauce and chicken seasoning. Marinade for about 30 minutes. Place the chicken on top of the tray.
4. Close the lid and flip the SmartSwitch to RAPID COOKER.
5. Select SPEEDI MEALS, set temperature to 390°F, and set time to 15 minutes. Press START/STOP to begin cooking (the unit will steam for approx. 10 minutes before crisping).
6. When cooking is complete, remove the chicken from the tray. Then use silicone-tipped tongs to grab the center handle and remove the tray from the unit. Transfer the rice and beans to a bowl, then top with the chicken and sesame seeds.

## CHICKEN BREAST WITH ARTICHOKES (SLOW COOK)

Prep Time: 8 minutes, Cook Time: 6 hours, Serves: 4 to 6

### INGREDIENTS:

- 8 (6-ounce / 170-g) boneless, skinless chicken breasts
- 2 (14-ounce / 397-g) BPA-free cans no-salt-added artichoke hearts, drained
- 2 red bell peppers, stemmed, seeded, and chopped
- 2 leeks, chopped
- 1 cup chicken stock
- ½ cup chopped flat-leaf parsley
- 3 garlic cloves, minced
- 2 tbsps. lemon juice
- 1 tsp. dried basil leaves

### DIRECTIONS:

1. Before getting started, be sure to remove the crisper tray.
2. Layer the leeks, garlic, artichoke hearts, bell peppers, chicken, stock, lemon juice, and basil in the bottom of the pot.
3. Close the lid and flip the SmartSwitch to AIRFRY/STOVETOP. Select SLOW COOK, set temperature to "Lo", and set time to 6 hours. Press START/STOP to begin cooking, until the chicken registers 165ºF on a food thermometer.
4. Garnish with the parsley and serve warm.

## THAI CHICKEN WITH GREENS AND PEPPERS (SLOW COOK)

Prep Time: 10 minutes, Cook Time: 8 hours, Serves: 6 to 8

### INGREDIENTS:

- 2 (16-ounce / 454-g) packages prepared collard greens
- 10 (4-ounce / 113-g) boneless, skinless chicken thighs
- 2 cups chopped kale
- 2 red chili peppers, minced
- 2 onions, chopped
- 1 cup canned coconut milk
- 1 cup chicken stock
- 6 garlic cloves, minced
- 1 lemongrass stalk
- 3 tbsps. freshly squeezed lime juice

### DIRECTIONS:

1. Before getting started, be sure to remove the crisper tray.
2. Mix the greens and kale and top with the onions, garlic, chili peppers, lemongrass, and chicken in the bottom of the pot. Pour in the chicken stock and coconut milk over all.
3. Close the lid and flip the SmartSwitch to AIRFRY/STOVETOP. Select SLOW COOK, set temperature to "Lo", and set time to 8 hours. Press START/STOP to begin cooking, until the chicken registers 165ºF on a food thermometer and the greens are soft.
4. Remove the lemongrass and discard. Gently stir in the lime juice and serve warm.

## SPICY MOLE CHICKEN BITES (SLOW COOK)

Prep Time: 10 minutes, Cook Time: 6 hours, Serves: 4

### INGREDIENTS:

- 6 (5-ounce / 142-g) boneless, skinless chicken breasts
- 4 large tomatoes, seeded and chopped
- 1 jalapeño pepper, minced
- 2 onions, chopped
- 6 garlic cloves, minced
- 2 dried red chilies, crushed
- ½ cup chicken stock
- 3 tbsps. cocoa powder
- 2 tbsps. chili powder
- 2 tbsps. coconut sugar

### DIRECTIONS:

1. Before getting started, be sure to remove the crisper tray.
2. Mix the onions, garlic, tomatoes, chili peppers, and jalapeño peppers in the bottom of the pot.
3. In a medium bowl, mix the cocoa powder, chili powder, coconut sugar, and chicken stock.
4. Slice the chicken breasts into 1-inch strips crosswise and place to the pot. Add the chicken stock mixture over all.
5. Close the lid and flip the SmartSwitch to AIRFRY/STOVETOP. Select SLOW COOK, set temperature to "Lo", and set time to 6 hours. Press START/STOP to begin cooking, until the chicken registers 165ºF on a food thermometer.
6. Serve warm with toothpicks or little plates and forks.

# BBQ CHICKEN (AIR FRY)

Prep Time: 10 minutes, Cook Time: 21 to 23 minutes, Serves: 4

### INGREDIENTS:

- cooking spray
- ⅓ cup no-salt-added tomato sauce
- 2 tbsps. low-sodium grainy mustard
- 2 tbsps. apple cider vinegar
- 1 tbsp. honey
- 2 garlic cloves, minced
- 1 jalapeño pepper, minced
- 3 tbsps. minced onion
- 4 (5-ounce / 142-g) low-sodium boneless, skinless chicken breasts

### DIRECTIONS:

1. Push in the legs on the Crisper Tray, then place the tray in the bottom of the pot. Spray the tray with cooking spray.
2. In a small bowl, toss together the tomato sauce, mustard, cider vinegar, garlic, jalapeño, honey, and onion.
3. Brush the chicken breasts with some sauce.
4. Close the lid and flip the SmartSwitch to AIRFRY/STOVETOP. Select AIRFRY, set temperature to 390°F, and set time to 23 minutes (unit will need to preheat for 5 minutes, so set an external timer if desired). Press START/STOP to begin cooking.
5. When the unit is preheated and the time reaches 18 minutes, place the chicken on the tray. Close the lid to begin cooking.
6. After 10 minutes, open the lid. Turn the chicken over and brush with more sauce. Close the lid to continue cooking.
7. Turn the chicken again; brush with more sauce. Cook for 3 to 5 minutes more, or until the chicken reaches an internal temperature of 165ºF on a meat thermometer. Discard any remaining sauce. Serve hot.

# AIR FRIED CHICKEN FAJITAS (AIR FRY)

Prep Time: 15 minutes, Cook Time: 15 minutes, Serves: 4

### INGREDIENTS:

- cooking spray
- 4 (5-ounce / 142-g) low-sodium boneless, skinless chicken breasts, cut into 4-by-½-inch strips
- 1 tbsp. freshly squeezed lemon juice
- 2 tsps. olive oil
- 2 tsps. chili powder
- 2 red bell peppers, sliced
- 4 low-sodium whole-wheat tortillas
- ⅓ cup nonfat sour cream
- 1 cup grape tomatoes, sliced

### DIRECTIONS:

1. Push in the legs on the Crisper Tray, then place the tray in the bottom of the pot. Spray the tray with cooking spray.
2. In a large bowl, mix the chicken, lemon juice, olive oil, and chili powder. Toss to coat.
3. Close the lid and flip the SmartSwitch to AIRFRY/STOVETOP. Select AIRFRY, set temperature to 375°F, and set time to 20 minutes (unit will need to preheat for 5 minutes, so set an external timer if desired). Press START/STOP to begin cooking.
4. When the unit is preheated and the time reaches 15 minutes, place the chicken on the tray. Close the lid to begin cooking, until the chicken reaches an internal temperature of 165ºF on a meat thermometer.
5. Assemble the fajitas with the tortillas, chicken, bell peppers, sour cream, and tomatoes. Serve immediately.

## CHICKEN STUFFED MUSHROOMS (STEAM&CRISP)

Prep: 10 minutes, Total Cook Time: 19 minutes, Steam: approx. 4 minutes, Cook: 15 minutes, Makes: 12 mushrooms

### INGREDIENTS:

- ½ cup water, for steaming
- 12 large fresh mushrooms, stems removed
- 1 cup chicken meat, cubed
- ½ lb. imitation crabmeat, flaked
- 2 cups butter
- Garlic powder, to taste
- 2 cloves garlic, peeled and minced
- Salt and black pepper, to taste
- 1 (8 oz.) package cream cheese, softened
- Crushed red pepper, to taste

### DIRECTIONS:

1. Pour ½ cup water into the pot. Push in the legs on the Crisper Tray, then place the tray in the bottom position in the pot.
2. Heat butter on medium heat in a nonstick skillet and add chicken.
3. Sauté for about 5 minutes and stir in the remaining ingredients except mushrooms.
4. Stuff this filling mixture in the mushroom caps on the tray.
5. Close the lid and flip the SmartSwitch to Rapid Cooker. Select STEAM & CRISP, set temperature to 375°F, and set time to 10 minutes. Press START/STOP to begin cooking (the unit will steam for approx. 4 minutes before crisping).
6. When cooking is complete, dish out to serve warm.

## CURRIED ORANGE HONEY CHICKEN (STEAM&CRISP)

Prep: 10 minutes, Total Cook Time: 19 minutes, Steam: approx. 4 minutes, Cook: 15 minutes, Serves: 4

### INGREDIENTS:

- ½ cup water, for steaming
- ¾ pound (340 g) boneless, skinless chicken thighs, cut into 1-inch pieces
- 1 yellow bell pepper, cut into 1½-inch pieces
- 1 small red onion, sliced
- Olive oil for misting
- ¼ cup chicken stock
- 2 tbsps. honey
- ¼ cup orange juice
- 1 tbsp. cornstarch
- 2 to 3 tsps. curry powder

### DIRECTIONS:

1. Pour ½ cup water into the pot. Pull out the legs on the Crisper Tray, then place the tray in the elevated position in the pot.
2. Put the chicken thighs, pepper, and red onion on the tray and mist with olive oil.
3. Close the lid and flip the SmartSwitch to Rapid Cooker. Select STEAM & CRISP, set temperature to 375°F, and set time to 15 minutes. Press START/STOP to begin cooking (the unit will steam for approx. 4 minutes before crisping).
4. After 5 minutes, open the lid and toss the chicken with tongs. Close the lid to continue cooking.
5. In a metal bowl, combine the stock, honey, orange juice, cornstarch, and curry powder, and mix well.
6. With 5 minutes remaining, open the lid and add the chicken and vegetables, stirring with the sauce. Close the lid to continue cooking, until the sauce is thickened and bubbly.
7. Serve warm.

## COCONUT CHICKEN MEATBALLS (STEAM&CRISP)

Prep: 10 minutes, Total Cook Time: 19 minutes, Steam: approx. 4 minutes, Cook: 15 minutes, Serves: 4

### INGREDIENTS:

- ½ cup water, for steaming
- 1 pound (454 g) ground chicken
- 2 scallions, finely chopped
- 1 cup chopped fresh cilantro leaves
- ¼ cup unsweetened shredded coconut
- 1 tbsp. hoisin sauce
- 1 tbsp. soy sauce
- 2 tsps. sriracha or other hot sauce
- 1 tsp. toasted sesame oil
- ½ tsp. kosher salt
- 1 tsp. black pepper

### DIRECTIONS:

1. Pour ½ cup water into the pot. Pull out the legs on the Crisper Tray, then place the tray in the elevated position in the pot.
2. In a large bowl, gently mix the chicken, scallions, cilantro, coconut, hoisin, soy sauce, sriracha, sesame oil, salt, and pepper until thoroughly combined (the mixture will be wet and sticky).
3. Place a sheet of parchment paper on the tray. Using a small scoop or teaspoon, drop rounds of the mixture in a single layer onto the parchment paper.
4. Close the lid and flip the SmartSwitch to Rapid Cooker. Select STEAM & CRISP, set temperature to 350°F, and set time to 15 minutes. Press START/STOP to begin cooking (the unit will steam for approx. 4 minutes before crisping).
5. With 5 minutes remaining, open the lid and flip the meatballs with tongs. Close the lid to continue cooking.
6. When cooking is complete, transfer the meatballs to a serving platter. Serve hot.

## CHEESY CHICKEN TACOS (STEAM&CRISP)

Prep: 10 minutes, Total Cook Time: 22 minutes, Steam: approx. 4 minutes, Cook: 18 minutes, Serves: 2 to 4

### INGREDIENTS:

- ½ cup water, for steaming
- 1 tsp. chili powder
- ½ tsp. ground cumin
- ½ tsp. garlic powder
- Salt and pepper, to taste
- Pinch cayenne pepper
- 1 pound (454 g) boneless, skinless chicken thighs, trimmed
- 1 tsp. vegetable oil
- 1 tomato, cored and chopped
- 2 tbsps. finely chopped red onion
- 2 tsps. minced jalapeño chile
- 1½ tsps. lime juice
- 6 to 12 (6-inch) corn tortillas, warmed
- 1 cup shredded iceberg lettuce
- 3 ounces (85 g) cheddar cheese, shredded (¾ cup)

### DIRECTIONS:

1. Pour ½ cup water into the pot. Pull out the legs on the Crisper Tray, then place the tray in the elevated position in the pot.
2. Combine chili powder, cumin, garlic powder, ½ tsp. salt, ¼ tsp. pepper, and cayenne in bowl. Pat chicken dry with paper towels, rub with oil, and sprinkle evenly with spice mixture. Place chicken on the tray.
3. Close the lid and flip the SmartSwitch to Rapid Cooker. Select STEAM & CRISP, set temperature to 375°F, and set time to 18 minutes. Press START/STOP to begin cooking (the unit will steam for approx. 4 minutes before crisping).
4. With 8 minutes remaining, open the lid and flip the chicken with tongs. Close the lid to continue cooking.
5. Meanwhile, combine tomato, onion, jalapeño, and lime juice in a bowl; season with salt and pepper to taste and set aside until ready to serve.
6. When cooking is complete, transfer chicken to a cutting board, let cool slightly, then shred into bite-size pieces using 2 forks. Serve chicken on warm tortillas, topped with salsa, lettuce, and cheddar.

## CHICKEN WITH PINEAPPLE AND PEACH (STEAM&CRISP)

Prep: 10 minutes, Total Cook Time: 20 minutes, Steam: approx. 4 minutes, Cook: 16 minutes, Serves: 4

### INGREDIENTS:

- ½ cup water, for steaming
- 1 pound (454 g) low-sodium boneless, skinless chicken breasts, cut into 1-inch pieces
- 1 medium red onion, chopped
- 1 (8-ounce / 227-g) can pineapple chunks, drained, ¼ cup juice reserved
- 1 tbsp. peanut oil or safflower oil
- 1 peach, peeled, pitted, and cubed
- 1 tbsp. cornstarch
- ½ tsp. ground ginger
- ¼ tsp. ground allspice
- Brown rice, cooked (optional)

### DIRECTIONS:

1. Pour ½ cup water into the pot. Pull out the legs on the Crisper Tray, then place the tray in the elevated position in the pot.
2. In a medium metal bowl, mix the chicken, red onion, pineapple, and peanut oil. Transfer the chicken mixture to the tray.
3. Close the lid and flip the SmartSwitch to Rapid Cooker. Select STEAM & CRISP, set temperature to 390°F, and set time to 16 minutes. Press START/STOP to begin cooking (the unit will steam for approx. 4 minutes before crisping).
4. With 6 minutes remaining, open the lid and add the peach. Close the lid to continue cooking.
5. Meanwhile, in a small bowl, whisk the reserved pineapple juice, the cornstarch, ginger, and allspice well.
6. With 3 minutes remaining, open the lid. Add the sauce to the chicken mixture and stir. Close the lid to continue cooking, until the chicken reaches an internal temperature of 165ºF on a meat thermometer and the sauce is slightly thickened.
7. Serve immediately over hot cooked brown rice, if desired.

## SIMPLE CHICKEN SHAWARMA (STEAM&CRISP)

Prep: 10 minutes, Total Cook Time: 16 minutes, Steam: approx. 4 minutes, Cook: 12 minutes, Serves: 4

### INGREDIENTS:

- ½ cup water, for steaming
- SHAWARMA SPICE:
- 2 tsps. dried oregano
- 1 tsp. ground cinnamon
- 1 tsp. ground cumin
- 1 tsp. ground coriander
- 1 tsp. kosher salt
- ½ tsp. ground allspice
- ½ tsp. cayenne pepper
- CHICKEN:
- 1 pound (454 g) boneless, skinless chicken thighs, cut into large bite-size chunks
- 2 tbsps. vegetable oil
- FOR SERVING:
- Tzatziki
- Pita bread

### DIRECTIONS:

1. For the shawarma spice: In a small bowl, combine the oregano, cayenne, cumin, coriander, salt, cinnamon, and allspice.
2. For the chicken: In a large bowl, toss together the chicken, vegetable oil, and shawarma spice to coat. Marinate at room temperature for 30 minutes or cover and refrigerate for up to 24 hours.
3. Pour ½ cup water into the pot. Pull out the legs on the Crisper Tray, then place the tray in the elevated position in the pot.
4. Place the chicken on the tray.
5. Close the lid and flip the SmartSwitch to Rapid Cooker. Select STEAM & CRISP, set temperature to 375°F, and set time to 12 minutes. Press START/STOP to begin cooking (the unit will steam for approx. 4 minutes before crisping).
6. With 5 minutes remaining, open the lid and flip the chicken with tongs. Close the lid to continue cooking, until the chicken reaches an internal temperature of 165ºF.
7. When cooking is complete, transfer the chicken to a serving platter. Serve with tzatziki and pita bread.

## CHICKEN THIGHS AND CREAMY GRITS (SPEEDI MEALS)

Prep: 15 minutes, Total Cook Time: 25 minutes, Steam: approx. 10 minutes, Cook: 15 minutes, Serves: 4

### INGREDIENTS:

- LEVEL 1 (BOTTOM OF POT)
- ¾ cup stone ground grits
- 1½ cups water
- ½ tsp. sea salt
- ½ cup cream cheese, at room temperature
- ¼ cup milk
- ½ tsp. garlic powder
- ¼ tsp. porcini powder
- LEVEL 2 (TRAY)
- 1 tsp. grated ginger

- 1½ lbs. chicken thighs
- 1 tbsp. five-spice powder
- ¼ cup soy sauce
- 3 tbsps. sesame oil
- Salt and pepper, to taste
- TOPPINGS:
- Chilli sauce
- Hummus
- Pesto

### DIRECTIONS:

1. Place all Level 1 ingredients in the pot and stir to combine.
2. Pull out the legs on the Crisper Tray, then place the tray in the elevated position in the pot.
3. In a large bowl, mix all the ingredients with the chicken thighs and marinade for 5 minutes. Place the chicken thighs on top of the tray.
4. Close the lid and flip the SmartSwitch to RAPID COOKER.
5. Select SPEEDI MEALS, set temperature to 390°F, and set time to 15 minutes. Press START/STOP to begin cooking (the unit will steam for approx. 10 minutes before crisping).
6. When cooking is complete, remove the chicken thighs from the tray. Then use silicone-tipped tongs to grab the center handle and remove the tray from the unit. Transfer the grits to a bowl, then top with the chicken thighs and toppings.
7. Serve warm.

## ASIAN CHICKEN WITH ZUCCHINI PENNE PASTA (SPEEDI MEALS)

Prep: 20 minutes, Total Cook Time: 25 minutes, Steam: approx. 10 minutes, Cook: 15 minutes, Serves: 4

### INGREDIENTS:

- LEVEL 1 (BOTTOM OF POT)
- 1 tbsp. butter
- 1 yellow onion, thinly sliced
- Salt and black pepper, to taste
- 2 garlic cloves, minced
- 1 zucchini, thinly sliced
- Pinch of dried basil
- 3½ cups water
- 2 tbsps. soy sauce
- 15 ounces (425 g) penne pasta

- 5 ounces (142 g) tomato paste
- LEVEL 2 (TRAY)
- 3 minced garlic cloves
- 1½ lbs. boneless chicken breasts
- 3 tbsps. soy sauce
- 1 tbsp. ginger slices
- TOPPINGS:
- Fresh herbs
- Salsa
- Guacamole

### DIRECTIONS:

1. Place all Level 1 ingredients in the pot and stir to combine.
2. Pull out the legs on the Crisper Tray, then place the tray in the elevated position in the pot.
3. Season the chicken breasts with garlic, soy sauce, and ginger slices. Place the chicken breasts on top of the tray.
4. Close the lid and flip the SmartSwitch to RAPID COOKER.
5. Select SPEEDI MEALS, set temperature to 390°F, and set time to 15 minutes. Press START/STOP to begin cooking (the unit will steam for approx. 10 minutes before crisping).
6. When cooking is complete, remove the chicken breasts from the tray. Then use silicone-tipped tongs to grab the center handle and remove the tray from the unit. Transfer the Zucchini Penne Pasta to a bowl, then top with the chicken breasts and toppings.

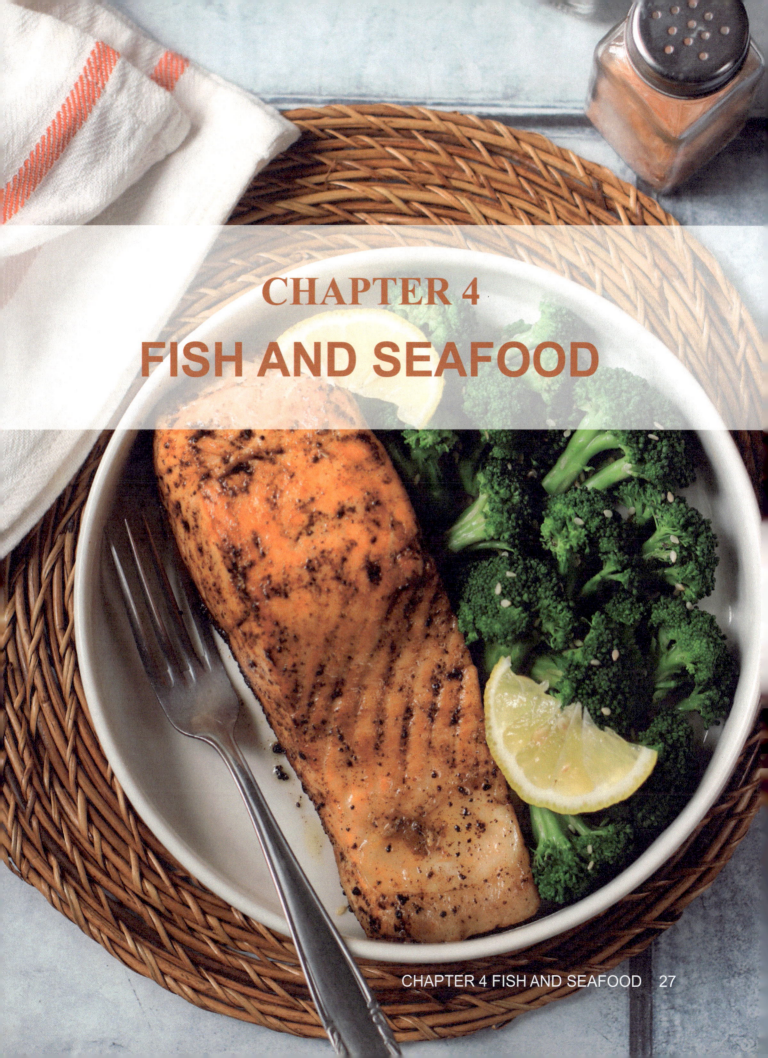

# CHAPTER 4
# FISH AND SEAFOOD

## DRUNKEN SHRIMP (SEAR/SAUTÉ)

Prep Time: 30 minutes, Cook Time: 10 minutes, Serves: 4

### INGREDIENTS:

- 2 cups Shaoxing rice wine
- 4 peeled fresh ginger slices, each about the size of a quarter
- 2 tbsps. dried goji berries (optional)
- 2 tsps. sugar
- 1 pound (454 g) jumbo shrimp, peeled and deveined, tails left on
- 2 tbsps. vegetable oil
- Kosher salt
- 2 tsps. cornstarch

### DIRECTIONS:

1. Before getting started, be sure to remove the Crisper Tray from the pot.
2. In a wide mixing bowl, stir together the rice wine, ginger, goji berries (if using), and sugar until the sugar is dissolved. Add the shrimp and cover. Marinate in the refrigerator for 20 to 30 minutes.
3. Flip the SmartSwitch to AIRFRY/STOVETOP. Select SEAR/SAUTÉ, choose "4". Press START/STOP to begin cooking.
4. Pour in the vegetable oil in the pot. Season the oil by adding a small pinch of salt, and swirl gently.
5. Add the shrimp and vigorously stir-fry, adding a pinch of salt as you flip and toss the shrimp around in the pot. Keep moving the shrimp around for about 3 minutes, until they just turn pink.
6. Stir the cornstarch into the reserved marinade and pour it over the shrimp. Toss the shrimp and coat with the marinade. It will thicken into a glossy sauce as it begins to boil, about another 5 minutes more.
7. Transfer the shrimp and goji berries to a platter, discard the ginger, and serve hot.

## BUTTERED SCALLOPS (AIR FRY)

Prep Time: 15 minutes, Cook Time: 6 minutes, Serves: 2

### INGREDIENTS:

- cooking spray
- ¾ pound sea scallops, cleaned and patted very dry
- 1 tbsp. butter, melted
- ½ tbsp. fresh thyme, minced
- Salt and black pepper, as required

### DIRECTIONS:

1. Push in the legs on the Crisper Tray, then place the tray in the bottom of the pot. Spray the tray with cooking spray.
2. Mix scallops, butter, thyme, salt, and black pepper in a bowl.
3. Close the lid and flip the SmartSwitch to AIRFRY/STOVETOP. Select AIRFRY, set temperature to 390°F, and set time to 11 minutes (unit will need to preheat for 5 minutes, so set an external timer if desired). Press START/STOP to begin cooking.
4. When the unit is preheated and the time reaches 6 minutes, place the scallops on the tray. Close the lid to begin cooking.
5. After 3 minutes, open the lid and flip the scallops with silicone-tipped tongs to ensure even cooking. Close the lid to continue cooking.
6. Dish out the scallops in a platter and serve hot.

## WHANGAREI STYLE MUSSELS (SEAR/SAUTÉ)

Prep Time: 20 minutes, Cook Time: 25 minutes, Serves: 4

### INGREDIENTS:

- 1 tbsp. butter
- 1 pound (454 g) mussels, cleaned and debearded
- 1 tbsp. olive oil
- 1 cup chopped green onions
- 2 tbsps. minced garlic
- 2 tbsps. minced shallots
- 1 tbsp. capers
- 3 cups canned tomato sauce
- 1 tbsp. Italian seasoning
- ½ tsp. red pepper flakes

### DIRECTIONS:

1. Before getting started, be sure to remove the Crisper Tray from the pot.
2. In a small bowl, mix together the rice wine, light soy, garlic, cornstarch, and sugar. Add the chicken and marinate for 10 minutes.
3. Flip the SmartSwitch to AIRFRY/STOVETOP. Select SEAR/SAUTÉ, choose "3". Press START/STOP to begin cooking.
4. Add the oil and butter in the pot. Sauté the shallots, garlic and capers for about 5 minutes.
5. Stir in the Italian herbs, tomato sauce and red pepper flakes and reduce the heat from "3" to "2".
6. Simmer, covered for about 10 minutes.
7. Stir in the mussels and increase the heat from "2" to "4".
8. Cook, covered for about 10 minutes.
9. Discard any unopened mussels from the pot.
10. Serve with a garnishing of the green onions.

## SALMON AND VEGGIES RATATOUILLE (SLOW COOK)

Prep Time: 20 minutes, Cook Time: 6½ hours, Serves: 8

### INGREDIENTS:

- 2 tbsps. olive oil
- 2 pounds (907 g) salmon fillets
- 5 large tomatoes, seeded and chopped
- 2 eggplants, peeled and chopped
- 2 cups sliced button mushrooms
- 2 red bell peppers, stemmed, seeded, and chopped
- 2 onions, chopped
- 5 garlic cloves, minced
- 1 tsp. dried herbes de Provence

### DIRECTIONS:

1. Before getting started, be sure to remove the crisper tray.
2. Mix the eggplants, tomatoes, mushrooms, onions, bell peppers, garlic, olive oil, and herbes de Provence in the bottom of the pot.
3. Close the lid and flip the SmartSwitch to AIRFRY/STOVETOP. Select SLOW COOK, set temperature to "Lo", and set time to 6 hours. Press START/STOP to begin cooking, until the vegetables are soft.
4. When the time is up, open the lid and place the salmon to the pot. Close the lid and cook on low for another 30 to 40 minutes, or until the salmon flakes when tested with a fork.
5. Serve warm.

## CARROT MÉLANGE WITH POACHED TROUT (SLOW COOK)

Prep Time: 15 minutes, Cook Time: 8½ hours, Serves: 8

### INGREDIENTS:

- 6 (5-ounce / 142-g) trout fillets
- 4 large orange carrots, peeled and sliced
- 3 purple carrots, peeled and sliced
- 3 yellow carrots, peeled and sliced
- ½ cup vegetable broth or fish stock

- 2 onions, chopped
- 4 garlic cloves, minced
- 1 bay leaf
- 1 tsp. dried marjoram leaves
- ½ tsp. salt

### DIRECTIONS:

1. Before getting started, be sure to remove the crisper tray.
2. Mix the carrots, onions, garlic, vegetable broth, marjoram, bay leaf, and salt in the bottom of the pot.
3. Close the lid and flip the SmartSwitch to AIRFRY/STOVETOP. Select SLOW COOK, set temperature to "Lo", and set time to 8 hours. Press START/STOP to begin cooking, until the carrots are soft.
4. When the time is up, open the lid. Remove the bay leaf and discard. Place the trout fillets to the pot. Close the lid and cook on low for another 20 to 30 minutes, or until the fish flakes when tested with a fork.
5. Enjoy!

## SOUTHERN FRENCH INSPIRED HALIBUT (SEAR/SAUTÉ)

Prep Time: 10 minutes, Cook Time: 15 minutes, Serves: 2

### INGREDIENTS:

- 1 tbsp. olive oil
- Salt and pepper to taste
- 2 (8-ounce / 227-g) halibut steaks
- 3 tbsps. capers, with liquid vinegar

- ½ cup white wine
- 1 tsp. chopped garlic
- ¼ cup butter

### DIRECTIONS:

1. Before getting started, be sure to remove the Crisper Tray from the pot.
2. Flip the SmartSwitch to AIRFRY/STOVETOP. Select SEAR/SAUTÉ, choose "4". Press START/STOP to begin cooking.
3. Pour in the olive oil in the pot. Sear the halibut steaks until browned from all sides.
4. Transfer the steaks into a bowl and keep aside.
5. Add the wine and with a spatula scrape any browned bits from the bottom.
6. Cook until the wine is almost absorbed.
7. Stir in the garlic, butter, capers, salt and pepper and simmer for 1 minute.
8. Stir in the steaks and cook until the fish flakes easily with a fork.
9. Serve fish immediately with the sauce from the pot poured over it.

## BREADED HAKE (STEAM&CRISP)

Prep: 15 minutes, Total Cook Time: 16 minutes, Steam: approx. 4 minutes, Cook: 12 minutes, Serves: 2

### INGREDIENTS:

- ½ cup water, for steaming
- 1 egg
- 4 ounces breadcrumbs

- 4 (6-ounces) hake fillets
- 1 lemon, cut into wedges
- 2 tbsps. vegetable oil

### DIRECTIONS:

1. Pour ½ cup water into the pot. Pull out the legs on the Crisper Tray, then place the tray in the elevated position in the pot.
2. Whisk the egg in a shallow bowl and mix breadcrumbs and oil in another bowl.
3. Dip hake fillets into the whisked egg and then, dredge in the breadcrumb mixture.
4. Arrange the hake fillets on the tray in a single layer.
5. Close the lid and flip the SmartSwitch to Rapid Cooker. Select STEAM & CRISP, set temperature to 450°F, and set time to 12 minutes. Press START/STOP to begin cooking (the unit will steam for approx. 4 minutes before crisping).
6. When cooking is complete, dish out the hake fillets onto serving plates and serve, garnished with lemon wedges.

## TUNA AND POTATO CAKES (STEAM&BAKE)

Prep: 20 minutes, Total Cook Time: 20 minutes, Steam: approx. 8 minutes, Cook: 12 minutes, Serves: 4

### INGREDIENTS:

- 1 cup water, for steaming
- 1 onion, chopped
- 1 green chili, seeded and finely chopped
- 2 (6-ounces) cans tuna, drained
- 1 medium boiled potato, mashed
- 1 cup celery
- 1 cup breadcrumbs
- 2 eggs
- ½ tbsp. olive oil
- 1 tbsp. fresh ginger, grated
- Salt, as required

### DIRECTIONS:

1. Pour 1 cup water into the pot. Push in the legs on the Crisper Tray, then place the tray in the bottom position in the pot.
2. Heat olive oil in a frying pan and add onions, ginger, and green chili.
3. Sauté for about 30 seconds and add the tuna.
4. Stir fry for about 3 minutes and dish out the tuna mixture onto a large bowl.
5. Add mashed potato, celery, and salt and mix well.
6. Make 4 equal-sized patties from the mixture.
7. Place the breadcrumbs in a shallow bowl and whisk the egg in another bowl.
8. Dredge each patty with breadcrumbs, then dip into egg and coat again with the breadcrumbs. Arrange tuna cakes on the tray.
9. Close the lid and flip the SmartSwitch to Rapid Cooker. Select STEAM & BAKE, set temperature to 390°F, and set time to 8 minutes. Press START/STOP to begin cooking (the unit will steam for approx. 8 minutes before baking).
10. With 4 minutes remaining, open the lid and flip the side with tongs. Close the lid to continue cooking.
11. Dish out the tuna cakes onto serving plates and serve warm.

## PRAWN BURGERS (STEAM&BAKE)

Prep: 20 minutes, Total Cook Time: 10 minutes, Steam: approx. 4 minutes, Cook: 6 minutes, Serves: 2

### INGREDIENTS:

- 1 cup water, for steaming
- ½ cup prawns, peeled, deveined and finely chopped
- ½ cup breadcrumbs
- 2-3 tbsps. onion, finely chopped
- 3 cups fresh baby greens
- ½ tsp. ginger, minced
- ½ tsp. garlic, minced
- ½ tsp. spices powder
- ½ tsp. ground cumin
- ¼ tsp. ground turmeric
- Salt and ground black pepper, as required

### DIRECTIONS:

1. Pour 1 cup water into the pot. Push in the legs on the Crisper Tray, then place the tray in the bottom position in the pot.
2. Mix the prawns, breadcrumbs, onion, ginger, garlic, and spices in a bowl.
3. Make small-sized patties from the mixture and transfer on the tray.
4. Close the lid and flip the SmartSwitch to Rapid Cooker. Select STEAM & BAKE, set temperature to 390°F, and set time to 6 minutes. Press START/STOP to begin cooking (the unit will steam for approx. 4 minutes before baking).
5. When cooking is complete, dish out in a platter.
6. Serve immediately warm alongside the baby greens.

## BREADED SHRIMP WITH LEMON (STEAM&CRISP)

Prep: 15 minutes, Total Cook Time: 20 minutes, Steam: approx. 8 minutes, Cook: 12 minutes, Serves: 3

### INGREDIENTS:

- ½ cup water, for steaming
- ½ cup plain flour
- 2 egg whites
- 1 cup breadcrumbs
- 1 pound large shrimp, peeled and deveined
- Salt and ground black pepper, as required
- ¼ tsp. lemon zest
- ¼ tsp. cayenne pepper
- ¼ tsp. red pepper flakes, crushed
- 2 tbsps. vegetable oil

### DIRECTIONS:

1. Pour ½ cup water into the pot. Push in the legs on the Crisper Tray, then place the tray in the bottom position in the pot.
2. Mix flour, salt, and black pepper in a shallow bowl.
3. Whisk the egg whites in a second bowl and mix the breadcrumbs, lime zest and spices in a third bowl.
4. Coat each shrimp with the flour, dip into egg whites and finally, dredge in the breadcrumbs.
5. Drizzle the shrimp evenly with olive oil and arrange half of the coated shrimps on the tray.
6. Close the lid and flip the SmartSwitch to Rapid Cooker. Select STEAM & CRISP, set temperature to 450°F, and set time to 6 minutes. Press START/STOP to begin cooking (the unit will steam for approx. 4 minutes before crisping).
7. Dish out the coated shrimps onto serving plates.
8. Repeat with the remaining shrimps and serve hot.

## GLAZED CALAMARI WITH PEA RICE (SPEEDI MEALS)

Prep: 25 minutes, Total Cook Time: 23 minutes, Steam: approx. 10 minutes, Cook: 13 minutes, Serves: 3

### INGREDIENTS:

- LEVEL 1 (BOTTOM OF POT)
- 1 tbsp. olive oil
- 1 clove garlic, minced
- ¼ cup chopped shallots
- 2 cups chicken broth
- 1½ cups basmati rice, rinsed
- 1 cup frozen peas
- ½ cup chopped carrots
- 2 tsps. curry powder
- Salt and ground black pepper, to taste

- LEVEL 2 (TRAY)
- ½ pound calamari tubes, cut into ¼ inch rings
- 1 cup club soda
- 1 cup flour
- ½ tbsp. red pepper flakes, crushed
- Salt and black pepper, to taste
- FOR SAUCE:
- ½ cup honey
- 2 tbsps. Sriracha sauce
- ¼ tsp. red pepper flakes, crushed

### DIRECTIONS:

1. Place all Level 1 ingredients in the pot and stir to combine.
2. Pull out the legs on the Crisper Tray, then place the tray in the elevated position in the pot.
3. Soak the calamari in the club soda in a bowl and keep aside for about 10 minutes.
4. Mix flour, red pepper flakes, salt, and black pepper in another bowl.
5. Drain the club soda from calamari and coat the calamari rings evenly with flour mixture.
6. Arrange calamari rings on top of the tray.
7. Close the lid and flip the SmartSwitch to RAPID COOKER.
8. Select SPEEDI MEALS, set temperature to 375°F, and set time to 13 minutes. Press START/STOP to begin cooking (the unit will steam for approx. 10 minutes before crisping).
9. With 2 minutes remaining, open the lid. Coat the calamari rings with the honey sauce. Close the lid to continue cooking.
10. When cooking is complete, remove the calamari rings from the tray. Then use silicone-tipped tongs to grab the center handle and remove the tray from the unit. Transfer the rice and vegetables to a bowl, then top with the calamari rings.
11. Serve hot.

## CREAMY BREADED SHRIMP (STEAM&CRISP)

Prep: 15 minutes, Total Cook Time: 18 minutes, Steam: approx. 8 minutes, Cook: 10 minutes, Serves: 3

### INGREDIENTS:

- ½ cup water, for steaming
- ¼ cup all-purpose flour
- 1 cup panko breadcrumbs
- 1 pound shrimp, peeled and deveined
- ½ cup mayonnaise
- ¼ cup sweet chili sauce
- 1 tbsp. Sriracha sauce

### DIRECTIONS:

1. Pour ½ cup water into the pot. Push in the legs on the Crisper Tray, then place the tray in the bottom position in the pot.
2. Place flour in a shallow bowl and mix the mayonnaise, chili sauce, and Sriracha sauce in another bowl.
3. Place the breadcrumbs in a third bowl.
4. Coat each shrimp with the flour, dip into mayonnaise mixture and finally, dredge in the breadcrumbs.
5. Arrange half of the coated shrimps on the tray.
6. Close the lid and flip the SmartSwitch to Rapid Cooker. Select STEAM & CRISP, set temperature to 450°F, and set time to 5 minutes. Press START/STOP to begin cooking (the unit will steam for approx. 4 minutes before crisping).
7. Dish out the shrimps onto serving plates.
8. Repeat with the remaining shrimps and serve hot.

## RANCH TILAPIA (STEAM&CRISP)

Prep: 15 minutes, Total Cook Time: 14 minutes, Steam: approx. 4 minutes, Cook: 10 minutes, Serves: 4

### INGREDIENTS:

- ½ cup water, for steaming
- ¾ cup cornflakes, crushed
- 2 eggs
- 4 (6-ounces) tilapia fillets
- 2½ tbsps. vegetable oil
- RANCH DRESSING:
- ½ cup dry buttermilk powder
- 1 tbsp. dried parsley
- 2 tsps. dried dill weed
- 1 tsp. freeze dried chives
- 1 tbsp. garlic powder
- 1 tbsp. onion powder
- 1 tsp. sea salt
- ½ tsp. ground black pepper

### DIRECTIONS:

1. Pour ½ cup water into the pot. Pull out the legs on the Crisper Tray, then place the tray in the elevated position in the pot.
2. Whisk the eggs in a shallow bowl.
3. Mix cornflakes, ranch dressing and olive oil in another bowl until a crumbly mixture is formed.
4. Dip the tilapia fillets into whisked eggs and dredge into the breadcrumb mixture.
5. Arrange tilapia fillets on the tray in a single layer.
6. Close the lid and flip the SmartSwitch to Rapid Cooker. Select STEAM & CRISP, set temperature to 450°F, and set time to 10 minutes. Press START/STOP to begin cooking (the unit will steam for approx. 4 minutes before crisping).
7. With 5 minutes remaining, open the lid and flip the tilapia fillets with tongs. Close the lid to continue cooking.
8. Dish out the tilapia fillets onto serving plates and serve hot.

## COCONUT CRUSTED SHRIMP (STEAM&CRISP)

Prep: 15 minutes, Total Cook Time: 24 minutes, Steam: approx. 8 minutes, Cook: 16 minutes, Serves: 3

### INGREDIENTS:

- ½ cup water, for steaming
- 8 ounces coconut milk
- ½ cup sweetened coconut, shredded
- ½ cup panko breadcrumbs
- 1 pound large shrimp, peeled and deveined
- Salt and black pepper, to taste

### DIRECTIONS:

1. Pour ½ cup water into the pot. Push in the legs on the Crisper Tray, then place the tray in the bottom position in the pot.
2. Place the coconut milk in a shallow bowl.
3. Mix coconut, breadcrumbs, salt, and black pepper in another bowl.
4. Dip each shrimp into coconut milk and finally, dredge in the coconut mixture.
5. Arrange half of the shrimps on the tray.
6. Close the lid and flip the SmartSwitch to Rapid Cooker. Select STEAM & CRISP, set temperature to 450°F, and set time to 8 minutes. Press START/STOP to begin cooking (the unit will steam for approx. 4 minutes before crisping).
7. Dish out the shrimps onto serving plates.
8. Repeat with the remaining shrimps to serve.

## CREAMY PASTA AND TUNA CAKES (SPEEDI MEALS)

Prep: 20 minutes, Total Cook Time: 25 minutes, Steam: approx. 10 minutes, Cook: 15 minutes, Serves: 4

### INGREDIENTS:

- LEVEL 1 (BOTTOM OF POT)
- 1 box (8 ounces) penne pasta
- 1½ cups water or chicken stock
- ½ cup grated goat cheese
- ¼ cup cream
- LEVEL 2 (TRAY)
- 2 (6-ounces) cans tuna, drained
- 1½ tbsps. almond flour
- 1½ tbsps. mayonnaise
- 1 tbsp. fresh lemon juice
- 1 tsp. dried dill
- 1 tsp. garlic powder
- ½ tsp. onion powder
- Pinch of salt and ground black pepper

### DIRECTIONS:

1. Place all Level 1 ingredients in the pot and stir to combine.
2. Pull out the legs on the Crisper Tray, then place the tray in the elevated position in the pot.
3. Mix the tuna, mayonnaise, almond flour, lemon juice, dill, and spices in a large bowl.
4. Make 4 equal-sized patties from the mixture and arrange on top of the tray.
5. Close the lid and flip the SmartSwitch to RAPID COOKER.
6. Select SPEEDI MEALS, set temperature to 350°F, and set time to 15 minutes. Press START/STOP to begin cooking (the unit will steam for approx. 10 minutes before crisping).
7. When cooking is complete, remove the tuna cakes from the tray. Then use silicone-tipped tongs to grab the center handle and remove the tray from the unit. Transfer the cheese pasta to a bowl, then top with the tuna cakes.
8. Serve warm.

## SCALLOPS WITH SPINACH AND QUINOA (SPEEDI MEALS)

Prep: 20 minutes, Total Cook Time: 16 minutes, Steam: approx. 10 minutes, Cook: 6 minutes, Serves: 2

### INGREDIENTS:

- LEVEL 1 (BOTTOM OF POT)
- 1 cup quinoa, rinsed
- 1½ cups water or stock
- Salt and ground black pepper, as required
- LEVEL 2 (TRAY)
- 1 (12-ounces) package frozen spinach, thawed and drained

- 8 jumbo sea scallops
- ¾ cup heavy whipping cream
- 1 tbsp. fresh basil, chopped
- Cooking spray
- Salt and ground black pepper, as required
- 1 tbsp. tomato paste
- 1 tsp. garlic, minced

### DIRECTIONS:

1. Place all Level 1 ingredients in the pot and stir to combine.
2. Pull out the legs on the Crisper Tray, then place the tray in the elevated position in the pot. Spray the tray with cooking spray.
3. Season the scallops evenly with salt and black pepper.
4. Mix cream, tomato paste, garlic, basil, salt, and black pepper in a bowl.
5. Place spinach on top of the tray, followed by seasoned scallops and top with the cream mixture.
6. Close the lid and flip the SmartSwitch to RAPID COOKER.
7. Select SPEEDI MEALS, set temperature to 400°F, and set time to 6 minutes. Press START/STOP to begin cooking (the unit will steam for approx. 10 minutes before crisping).
8. When cooking is complete, remove the scallops and spinach from the tray. Then use silicone-tipped tongs to grab the center handle and remove the tray from the unit. Transfer the quinoa to a bowl, then top with the scallops and spinach.
9. Serve hot.

## PESTO HALIBUT AND BROCCOLI PASTA (SPEEDI MEALS)

Prep: 18 minutes, Total Cook Time: 25 minutes, Steam: approx. 10 minutes, Cook: 15 minutes, Serves: 4

### INGREDIENTS:

- LEVEL 1 (BOTTOM OF POT)
- 2 cups water
- ½ pound (227 g) pasta
- ½ cup broccoli
- ½ cup half and half
- 8 ounces (227 g) grated Cheddar cheese
- Salt, to taste

- LEVEL 2 (TRAY)
- 2 tbsps. extra virgin olive oil
- 1 tbsp. freshly squeezed lemon juice
- 1 cup basil leaves
- 2 garlic cloves, minced
- 4 halibut fillets
- Salt and pepper, to taste

### DIRECTIONS:

1. Place all Level 1 ingredients in the pot and stir to combine.
2. Pull out the legs on the Crisper Tray, then place the tray in the elevated position in the pot.
3. In a food processor, pulse the basil, olive oil, garlic, and lemon juice until coarse. Sprinkle salt and pepper for seasoning.
4. Spread pesto sauce over halibut fillets. Place the halibut fillets on top of the tray.
5. Close the lid and flip the SmartSwitch to RAPID COOKER.
6. Select SPEEDI MEALS, set temperature to 350°F, and set time to 15 minutes. Press START/STOP to begin cooking (the unit will steam for approx. 10 minutes before crisping).
7. When cooking is complete, remove the halibut fillets from the tray. Then use silicone-tipped tongs to grab the center handle and remove the tray from the unit. Transfer the pasta and broccoli to a bowl, then top with the halibut fillets.

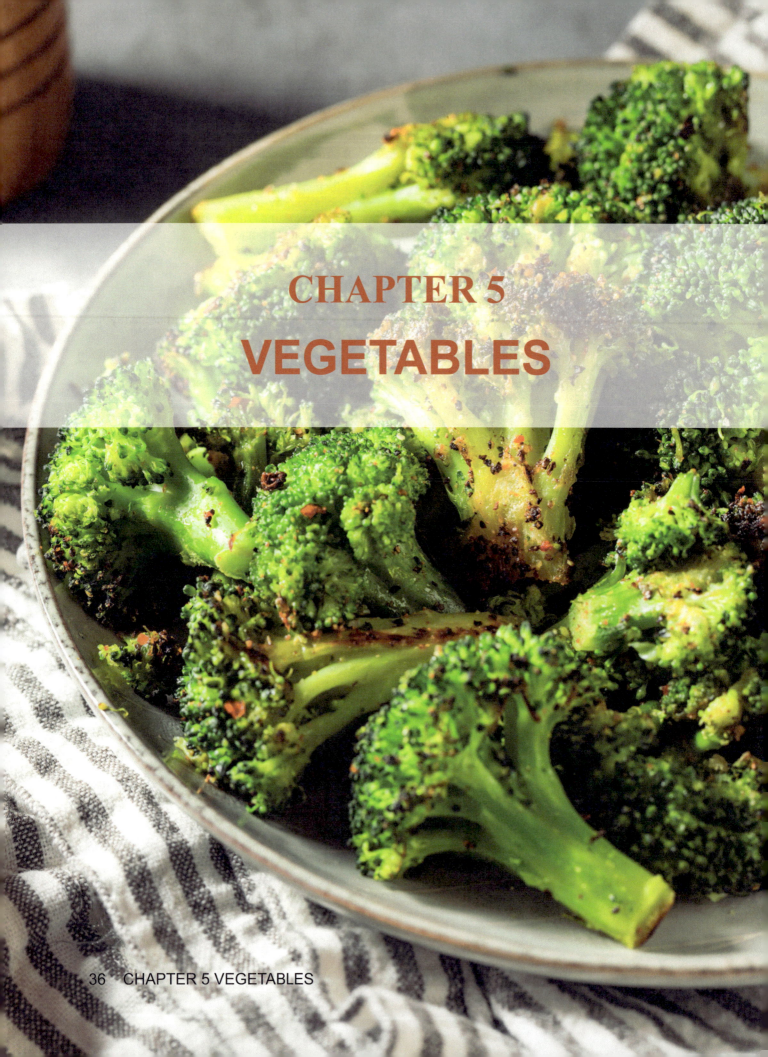

# CHAPTER 5

# VEGETABLES

## SESAME ASPARAGUS (SEAR/SAUTÉ)

Prep Time: 5 minutes, Cook Time: 6 minutes, Serves: 4

### INGREDIENTS:

- 2 tbsps. light soy sauce
- 1 tsp. sugar
- 1 tbsp. vegetable oil
- 2 large garlic cloves, coarsely chopped
- 2 pounds (907 g) asparagus, trimmed and cut diagonally into 2-inch-long pieces
- Kosher salt
- 2 tbsps. sesame oil
- 1 tbsp. toasted sesame seeds

### DIRECTIONS:

1. Before getting started, be sure to remove the Crisper Tray from the pot.
2. In a small bowl, stir the light soy and sugar together until the sugar dissolves. Set aside.
3. Flip the SmartSwitch to AIRFRY/STOVETOP. Select SEAR/SAUTÉ, choose "4". Press START/STOP to begin cooking.
4. Pour in the vegetable oil in the pot. Add the garlic and sauté until fragrant, about 10 seconds.
5. Add the asparagus and sauté until crisp-tender, about 4 minutes, seasoning with a small pinch of salt while sautéing. Add the soy sauce mixture and toss to coat the asparagus, cooking for about 1 minute more.
6. Drizzle the sesame oil over the asparagus and transfer to a serving bowl. Garnish with the sesame seeds and serve hot.

## BLISTERED SHISHITO PEPPERS (AIR FRY)

Prep Time: 10 minutes, Cook Time: 8 minutes, Serves: 4

### INGREDIENTS:

- DIPPING SAUCE:
- 1 cup sour cream
- 2 tbsps. fresh lemon juice
- 1 clove garlic, minced
- 1 green onion (white and green parts), finely chopped

- PEPPERS:
- 8 ounces (227 g) shishito peppers
- 1 tbsp. vegetable oil
- 1 tsp. toasted sesame oil
- Kosher salt and black pepper, to taste
- ¼ to ½ tsp. red pepper flakes
- ½ tsp. toasted sesame seeds

### DIRECTIONS:

1. Push in the legs on the Crisper Tray, then place the tray in the bottom of the pot. Spray the tray with cooking spray.
2. In a small bowl, mix all the ingredients for the dipping sauce to combine well. Cover and refrigerate until serving time.
3. In a medium bowl, stir the peppers with the vegetable oil.
4. Close the lid and flip the SmartSwitch to AIRFRY/STOVETOP. Select AIRFRY, set temperature to 350°F, and set time to 13 minutes (unit will need to preheat for 5 minutes, so set an external timer if desired). Press START/STOP to begin cooking.
5. When the unit is preheated and the time reaches 8 minutes, place the peppers on the tray. Close the lid to begin cooking.
6. After 4 minutes, open the lid and toss the peppers with silicone-tipped tongs to ensure even cooking. Close the lid to continue cooking.
7. When cooking is complete, transfer the peppers to a serving bowl. Pour the sesame oil and toss to coat well. Sprinkle with salt and pepper. Place the red pepper and sesame seeds and toss again.
8. Serve hot with the dipping sauce.

## ITALIAN BEETS AND TOMATO (SLOW COOK)

Prep Time: 17 minutes, Cook Time: 6 hours, Serves: 10

### INGREDIENTS:

- 2 tbsps. olive oil
- 10 medium beets, peeled and sliced
- 4 large tomatoes, seeded and chopped
- 2 onions, chopped

- 4 garlic cloves, minced
- 1 tsp. dried oregano leaves
- 1 tsp. dried basil leaves
- ½ tsp. salt

### DIRECTIONS:

1. Before getting started, be sure to remove the crisper tray.
2. Mix the beets, tomatoes, onions, and garlic in the bottom of the pot.
3. Add the olive oil and sprinkle with the dried herbs and salt. Toss to mix well.
4. Close the lid and flip the SmartSwitch to AIRFRY/STOVETOP. Select SLOW COOK, set temperature to "Lo", and set time to 6 hours. Press START/STOP to begin cooking, until the beets are soft.
5. Serve warm.

## SIMPLE ROASTED ROOT VEGETABLES (SLOW COOK)

Prep Time: 17 minutes, Cook Time: 7 hours, Serves: 12

### INGREDIENTS:

- 3 tbsps. olive oil
- 6 carrots, cut into 1-inch chunks
- 6 Yukon Gold potatoes, cut into chunks
- 2 sweet potatoes, peeled and cut into chunks
- 4 parsnips, peeled and cut into chunks

- 2 yellow onions, each cut into 8 wedges
- 8 whole garlic cloves, peeled
- 1 tsp. dried thyme leaves
- ½ tsp. salt
- ⅛ tsp. freshly ground black pepper

### DIRECTIONS:

1. Before getting started, be sure to remove the crisper tray.
2. Mix all the ingredients in the bottom of the pot.
3. Close the lid and flip the SmartSwitch to AIRFRY/STOVETOP. Select SLOW COOK, set temperature to "Lo", and set time to 7 hours. Press START/STOP to begin cooking, until the vegetables are soft.
4. Serve warm.

## QUINOA WITH MUSHROOM AND CARROT (SLOW COOK)

Prep Time: 8 minutes, Cook Time: 6 hours, Serves: 8 to 10

### INGREDIENTS:

- 2 cups quinoa, rinsed and drained
- 4 cups low-sodium vegetable broth
- 1 cup sliced cremini mushrooms
- 2 carrots, peeled and sliced
- 2 onions, chopped

- 3 garlic cloves, minced
- 1 tsp. dried marjoram leaves
- ½ tsp. salt
- ⅛ tsp. freshly ground black pepper

### DIRECTIONS:

1. Before getting started, be sure to remove the crisper tray.
2. Mix all of the ingredients in the bottom of the pot.
3. Close the lid and flip the SmartSwitch to AIRFRY/STOVETOP. Select SLOW COOK, set temperature to "Lo", and set time to 6 hours. Press START/STOP to begin cooking, until the quinoa and vegetables are soft.
4. Stir in the mixture and serve warm.

## TEX-MEX SWEET POTATOES AND PEPPERS (SLOW COOK)

Prep Time: 18 minutes, Cook Time: 8 hours, Serves: 8 to 10

### INGREDIENTS:

- 2 tbsps. olive oil
- 5 large sweet potatoes, peeled and chopped
- 2 jalapeño peppers, minced
- 3 onions, chopped
- 5 garlic cloves, minced

- ⅓ cup vegetable broth
- 1 tbsp. chili powder
- 1 tsp. ground cumin
- ½ tsp. salt

### DIRECTIONS:

1. Before getting started, be sure to remove the crisper tray.
2. Mix all of the ingredients in the bottom of the pot.
3. Close the lid and flip the SmartSwitch to AIRFRY/STOVETOP. Select SLOW COOK, set temperature to "Lo", and set time to 8 hours. Press START/STOP to begin cooking.
4. Stir in the mixture gently but thoroughly and serve warm.

## SIMPLE CURRIED SQUASH (SLOW COOK)

Prep Time: 17 minutes, Cook Time: 6 hours, Serves: 6 to 8

### INGREDIENTS:

- 3 acorn squashes, peeled, seeded, and cut into 1-inch pieces
- 1 large butternut squash, peeled, seeded, and cut into 1-inch pieces
- ⅓ cup freshly squeezed orange juice
- 2 onions, finely chopped

- 5 garlic cloves, minced
- 1 tbsp. curry powder
- ½ tsp. salt

### DIRECTIONS:

1. Before getting started, be sure to remove the crisper tray.
2. Mix all of the ingredients in the bottom of the pot.
3. Close the lid and flip the SmartSwitch to AIRFRY/STOVETOP. Select SLOW COOK, set temperature to "Lo", and set time to 6 hours. Press START/STOP to begin cooking, until the squash is tender when pierced with a fork.
4. Serve warm.

## POTATOES WITH ZUCCHINIS (AIR FRY)

Prep Time: 10 minutes, Cook Time: 25 minutes, Serves: 6

### INGREDIENTS:

- cooking spray
- 2 potatoes, peeled and cubed
- 4 carrots, cut into chunks
- 1 head broccoli, cut into florets

- 4 zucchinis, sliced thickly
- Salt and ground black pepper, to taste
- ¼ cup olive oil
- 1 tbsp. dry onion powder

### DIRECTIONS:

1. Push in the legs on the Crisper Tray, then place the tray in the bottom of the pot. Spray the tray with cooking spray.
2. In a large bowl, add all the ingredients and combine well.
3. Close the lid and flip the SmartSwitch to AIRFRY/STOVETOP. Select AIRFRY, set temperature to 390°F, and set time to 30 minutes (unit will need to preheat for 5 minutes, so set an external timer if desired). Press START/STOP to begin cooking.
4. When the unit is preheated and the time reaches 25 minutes, place the vegetables on the tray. Close the lid to begin cooking.
5. After 10 minutes, open the lid and toss the vegetables with silicone-tipped tongs to ensure even cooking. Close the lid to continue cooking.
6. Serve warm.

## HONEY-GLAZED TURNIPS AND FENNEL (SLOW COOK)

Prep Time: 10 minutes, Cook Time: 7 hours, Serves: 8 to 10

### INGREDIENTS:

- 4 pounds (1.8 kg) turnips, peeled and sliced
- 4 cups chopped turnip greens
- 1 bulk fennel, cored and chopped
- ¼ cup honey
- ¼ cup vegetable broth
- 2 garlic cloves, minced
- ½ tsp. salt

### DIRECTIONS:

1. Before getting started, be sure to remove the crisper tray.
2. Mix all of the ingredients in the bottom of the pot.
3. Close the lid and flip the SmartSwitch to AIRFRY/STOVETOP. Select SLOW COOK, set temperature to "Lo", and set time to 7 hours. Press START/STOP to begin cooking, until the turnips are tender when pierced with a fork and the greens are tender too.
4. Serve warm.

## BAKED EGGPLANT WITH BACON (BAKE&ROAST)

Prep Time: 15 minutes, Cook Time: 30 minutes, Serves: 2

### INGREDIENTS:

- 2 eggplants, cut in half lengthwise
- ½ cup cheddar cheese, shredded
- ½ can (7.5 oz.) chili without beans
- 2 tbsps. cooked bacon bits
- Fresh scallions, thinly sliced
- 2 tsps. kosher salt
- 2 tbsps. sour cream

### DIRECTIONS:

1. Push in the legs on the Crisper Tray, then place the tray in the bottom of the pot. Spray the tray with cooking spray.
2. Close the lid and flip the SmartSwitch to AIRFRY/STOVETOP. Select BAKE & ROAST, set temperature to 390°F, and set time to 35 minutes (unit will need to preheat for 5 minutes, so set an external timer if desired). Press START/STOP to begin cooking.
3. When the unit is preheated and the time reaches 30 minutes, place the eggplants with their skin side down on the tray. Close the lid to begin cooking.
4. With 5 minutes remaining, open the lid. Top each half with salt, chili and cheddar cheese. Close the lid to continue cooking.
5. Dish out in a bowl. Garnish with sour cream, bacon bits and scallions to serve.

## EASY THREE-BEAN MEDLEY (SLOW COOK)

Prep Time: 16 minutes, Cook Time: 8 hours, Serves: 10

### INGREDIENTS:

- 1¼ cups dried black beans, rinsed and drained
- 1¼ cups dried kidney beans, rinsed and drained
- 1¼ cups dried black-eyed peas, rinsed and drained
- 2 carrots, peeled and chopped
- 6 cups low-sodium vegetable broth
- 1½ cups water
- 1 onion, chopped
- 1 leek, chopped
- 2 garlic cloves, minced
- ½ tsp. dried thyme leaves

### DIRECTIONS:

1. Before getting started, be sure to remove the crisper tray.
2. Mix all of the ingredients in the bottom of the pot.
3. Close the lid and flip the SmartSwitch to AIRFRY/STOVETOP. Select SLOW COOK, set temperature to "Lo", and set time to 8 hours. Press START/STOP to begin cooking, until the beans are soft and the liquid is absorbed.
4. Serve warm.

# CRISPY ZUCCHINI FRIES (AIR FRY)

Prep Time: 10 minutes, Cook Time: 15 minutes, Serves: 4

### INGREDIENTS:

- cooking spray
- 1 pound zucchini, sliced into 2½-inch sticks
- ¾ cup panko breadcrumbs
- Salt, to taste

### DIRECTIONS:

1. Push in the legs on the Crisper Tray, then place the tray in the bottom of the pot. Spray the tray with cooking spray.
2. Season zucchini with salt and keep aside for about 10 minutes.
3. Place breadcrumbs in a shallow dish and coat zucchini fries in it.
4. Close the lid and flip the SmartSwitch to AIRFRY/STOVETOP. Select AIRFRY, set temperature to 390°F, and set time to 20 minutes (unit will need to preheat for 5 minutes, so set an external timer if desired). Press START/STOP to begin cooking.
5. When the unit is preheated and the time reaches 15 minutes, place the zucchini fries on the tray. Close the lid to begin cooking.
6. After 8 minutes, open the lid and toss the zucchini fries with silicone-tipped tongs to ensure even cooking. Close the lid to continue cooking.
7. Dish out and serve warm.

# CRISPY JICAMA FRIES (AIR FRY)

Prep Time: 5 minutes, Cook Time: 20 minutes, Serves: 1

### INGREDIENTS:

- cooking spray
- 1 small jicama, peeled
- ¼ tsp. onion powder
- ¾ tsp. chili powder
- ¼ tsp. garlic powder
- ¼ tsp. ground black pepper

### DIRECTIONS:

1. Push in the legs on the Crisper Tray, then place the tray in the bottom of the pot. Spray the tray with cooking spray.
2. To make the fries, cut the jicama into matchsticks of the desired thickness.
3. In a bowl, toss them with the onion powder, chili powder, garlic powder, and black pepper to coat.
4. Close the lid and flip the SmartSwitch to AIRFRY/STOVETOP. Select AIRFRY, set temperature to 350°F, and set time to 25 minutes (unit will need to preheat for 5 minutes, so set an external timer if desired). Press START/STOP to begin cooking.
5. When the unit is preheated and the time reaches 20 minutes, place the fries on the tray. Close the lid to begin cooking.
6. After 10 minutes, open the lid and toss the fries with silicone-tipped tongs to ensure even cooking. Close the lid to continue cooking. The fries are ready when they are hot and golden.
7. Serve immediately.

## RADISH STICKS (AIR FRY)

Prep Time: 10 minutes, Cook Time: 12 minutes, Serves: 2

**INGREDIENTS:**

- cooking spray
- 1 large radish, peeled and cut into sticks
- 1 tbsp. fresh rosemary, finely chopped
- 1 tbsp. olive oil
- 2 tsps. sugar
- ¼ tsp. cayenne pepper
- Salt and black pepper, as needed

**DIRECTIONS:**

1. Push in the legs on the Crisper Tray, then place the tray in the bottom of the pot. Spray the tray with cooking spray.
2. Mix radish with all other ingredients in a bowl until well combined.
3. Close the lid and flip the SmartSwitch to AIRFRY/STOVETOP. Select AIRFRY, set temperature to 390°F, and set time to 17 minutes (unit will need to preheat for 5 minutes, so set an external timer if desired). Press START/STOP to begin cooking.
4. When the unit is preheated and the time reaches 12 minutes, place the radish sticks on the tray. Close the lid to begin cooking.
5. After 7 minutes, open the lid and flip the radish sticks with silicone-tipped tongs to ensure even cooking. Close the lid to continue cooking.
6. Dish out and serve warm.

## BROCCOLI BITES (STEAM&CRISP)

Prep: 15 minutes, Total Cook Time: 16 minutes, Steam: approx. 4 minutes, Cook: 12 minutes, Makes: 10 bites

**INGREDIENTS:**

- ½ cup water, for steaming
- 2 cups broccoli florets
- 2 eggs, beaten
- 1¼ cups cheddar cheese, grated
- ¼ cup Parmesan cheese, grated
- 1¼ cups panko breadcrumbs
- Salt and black pepper, to taste

**DIRECTIONS:**

1. Pour ½ cup water into the pot. Push in the legs on the Crisper Tray, then place the tray in the bottom position in the pot.
2. Mix broccoli with rest of the ingredients and mix until well combined.
3. Make small equal-sized balls from mixture and arrange these balls in a baking pan. Refrigerate for about half an hour and then transfer into the tray.
4. Close the lid and flip the SmartSwitch to Rapid Cooker. Select STEAM & CRISP, set temperature to 400°F, and set time to 12 minutes. Press START/STOP to begin cooking (the unit will steam for approx. 4 minutes before crisping).
5. With 6 minutes remaining, open the lid and flip the broccoli with tongs. Close the lid to continue cooking.
6. Dish out to serve warm.

## GREEN BEANS WITH SHALLOT (STEAM&CRISP)

Prep: 10 minutes, Total Cook Time: 14 minutes, Steam: approx. 4 minutes, Cook: 10 minutes, Serves: 4

**INGREDIENTS:**

* ½ cup water, for steaming
* 1½ pounds (680 g) French green beans, stems removed and blanched
* 1 tbsp. salt
* ½ pound (227 g) shallots, peeled and cut into quarters
* ½ tsp. ground white pepper
* 2 tbsps. olive oil

**DIRECTIONS:**

1. Pour ½ cup water into the pot. Push in the legs on the Crisper Tray, then place the tray in the bottom position in the pot.
2. Coat the vegetables evenly with the rest of the ingredients in a bowl. Then transfer the vegetables to the tray.
3. Close the lid and flip the SmartSwitch to Rapid Cooker. Select STEAM & CRISP, set temperature to 375°F, and set time to 10 minutes. Press START/STOP to begin cooking (the unit will steam for approx. 4 minutes before crisping).
4. With 5 minutes remaining, open the lid and toss the vegetables with tongs. Close the lid to continue cooking.
5. When cooking is complete, use tongs to remove the vegetables from the tray and serve hot.

## CRISPY CAULIFLOWER POPPERS (STEAM&CRISP)

Prep: 10 minutes, Total Cook Time: 22 minutes, Steam: approx. 4 minutes, Cook: 18 minutes, Serves: 4

**INGREDIENTS:**

* ½ cup water, for steaming
* 1 large egg white
* ¾ cup panko breadcrumbs
* 4 cups cauliflower florets
* 3 tbsps. ketchup
* 2 tbsps. hot sauce

**DIRECTIONS:**

1. Pour ½ cup water into the pot. Push in the legs on the Crisper Tray, then place the tray in the bottom position in the pot.
2. Mix together the egg white, ketchup, and hot sauce in a bowl until well combined.
3. Stir in the cauliflower florets and generously coat with marinade.
4. Place breadcrumbs in a shallow dish and dredge the cauliflower florets in it.
5. Arrange the cauliflower florets on the the tray.
6. Close the lid and flip the SmartSwitch to Rapid Cooker. Select STEAM & CRISP, set temperature to 425°F, and set time to 18 minutes. Press START/STOP to begin cooking (the unit will steam for approx. 4 minutes before crisping).
7. With 8 minutes remaining, open the lid and flip the cauliflower florets with tongs. Close the lid to continue cooking.
8. Dish out and serve warm.

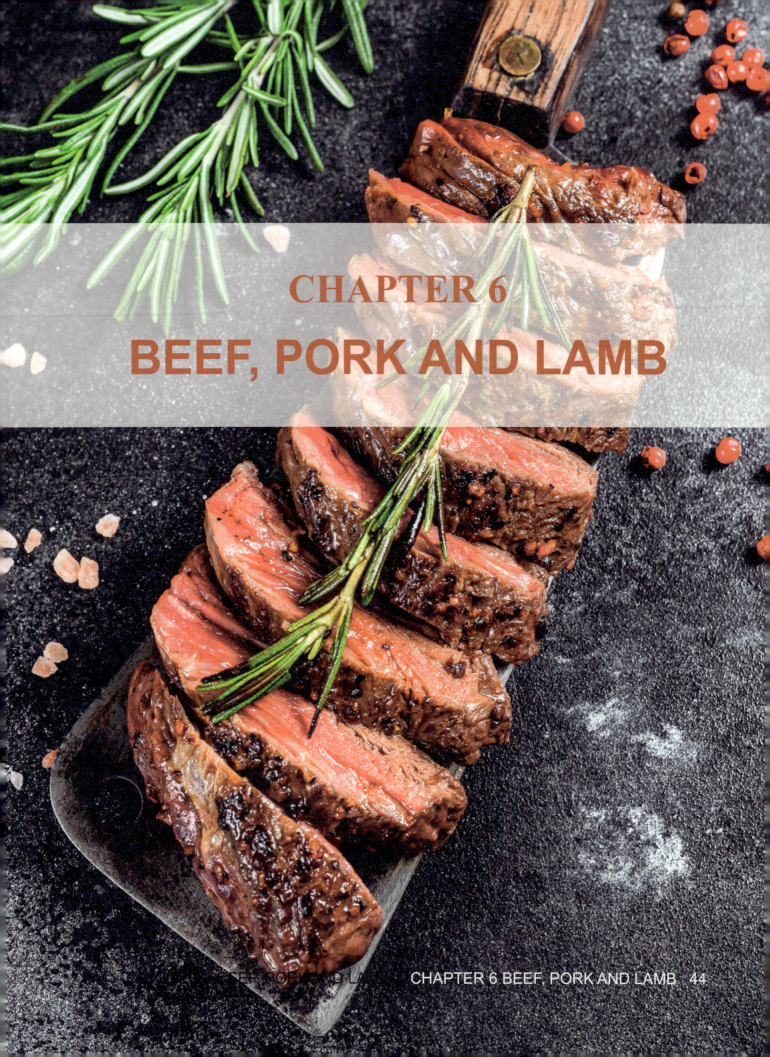

# CHAPTER 6
# BEEF, PORK AND LAMB

## MONGOLIAN BEEF (SEAR/SAUTÉ)

Prep Time: 15 minutes, Cook Time: 10 minutes, Serves: 4

### INGREDIENTS:

- 2 tbsps. Shaoxing rice wine
- 1 tbsp. dark soy sauce
- 1 tbsp. cornstarch, divided
- ¾ pound (340 g) flank steak, cut against the grain into ¼-inch-thick slices
- ¼ cup low-sodium chicken broth
- 1 tbsp. light brown sugar
- 1 cup vegetable oil
- 4 or 5 whole dried red Chinese chilies
- 4 garlic cloves, coarsely chopped
- 1 tsp. peeled finely minced fresh ginger
- ½ yellow onion, thinly sliced
- 2 tbsps. coarsely chopped fresh cilantro

### DIRECTIONS:

1. Before getting started, be sure to remove the Crisper Tray from the pot.
2. In a mixing bowl, stir together the rice wine, dark soy, and 1 tbsp. of cornstarch. Add the sliced flank steak and toss to coat. Set aside and marinate for 10 minutes.
3. Flip the SmartSwitch to AIRFRY/STOVETOP. Select SEAR/SAUTÉ, choose "4". Press START/STOP to begin cooking.
4. Pour the oil into the pot and bring it to 375ºF. You can tell the oil is at the right temperature when you dip the end of a wooden spoon into the oil. If the oil bubbles and sizzles around it, the oil is ready.
5. Lift the beef from the marinade, reserving the marinade. Add the beef to the oil and sauté for 2 to 3 minutes, until it develops a golden crust. Using a skimmer, transfer the beef to a clean bowl and set aside. Add the chicken broth and brown sugar to the marinade bowl and stir to combine.
6. Pour out all but 1 tbsp. of oil from the pot. Add the chili peppers, garlic, and ginger. Allow the aromatics to sizzle in the oil for about 10 seconds, swirling gently.
7. Add the onion and sear for 1 to 2 minutes, or until the onion is soft and translucent. Add the chicken broth mixture and toss to combine. Simmer for about 2 minutes, then add the beef and toss everything together for another 30 seconds.
8. Transfer to a platter, garnish with the cilantro, and serve hot.

## SUGAR SNAP AND BEEF (SEAR/SAUTÉ)

Prep Time: 25 minutes, Cook Time: 19 minutes, Serves: 6

### INGREDIENTS:

- 1 (14-ounce / 397-g) can jellied cranberry sauce
- 3 tbsps. olive oil
- 2 tbsps. lemon juice
- 1 tbsp. minced garlic
- ¾ cup broccoli florets
- 2 pounds (907 g) cubed beef stew meat
- ¾ cup sliced carrot
- 1 tsp. ground ginger
- ¾ cup sugar snap peas
- ¾ cup sliced onion

### DIRECTIONS:

1. Before getting started, be sure to remove the Crisper Tray from the pot.
2. In a small mixing bowl, combine the lemon juice with cranberry sauce.
3. Flip the SmartSwitch to AIRFRY/STOVETOP. Select SEAR/SAUTÉ, choose "4". Press START/STOP to begin cooking.
4. Add a splash of oil in the pot. Place the broccoli, carrot, snap peas, and onion. Sauté them for 6 minutes. Set the mixture aside.
5. Add oil in the pot. Sauté the garlic for 1 minutes. Add the beef and cook for 6 minutes.
6. Place the cooked veggies with ginger and cranberry sauce mixture. Cook them for 6 minutes. Serve warm.

## LAMB BATNA (SEAR/SAUTÉ)

Prep Time: 10 minutes, Cook Time: 1 hour, Serves: 8

### INGREDIENTS:

- 2½ pounds (1.1 kg) lamb, cubed
- 1 pear, peeled and cubed
- 3 tbsps. butter
- ¼ cup orange juice
- ½ tsp. ground cinnamon
- 1 tsp. orange blossom water
- 3 cups water
- ¼ cup sugar
- 16 prunes, soaked and drained
- 2 tbsps. raisins
- 2 tbsps. almonds

### DIRECTIONS:

1. Before getting started, be sure to remove the Crisper Tray from the pot.
2. Flip the SmartSwitch to AIRFRY/STOVETOP. Select SEAR/SAUTÉ, choose "3". Press START/STOP to begin cooking.
3. Melt the butter in the pot.
4. Sauté the lamb for 6 minutes. Stir in the cinnamon with sugar and water.
5. Sauté them for 32 minutes while stirring often with the lid on.
6. Stir in the prunes, raisins, almonds, pear, and orange blossom water.
7. Cook them for an extra 16 minutes until the sauce becomes thick.
8. Stir in the orange juice and cook it for 5 minutes.
9. Adjust the seasoning of your stew then serve it hot.

## HOISIN PORK (SEAR/SAUTÉ)

Prep Time: 15 minutes, Cook Time: 6 minutes, Serves: 4

### INGREDIENTS:

- 2 tsps. Shaoxing rice wine
- 2 tsps. light soy sauce
- ½ tsp. chili paste
- ¾ pound (340 g) boneless pork loin, thinly sliced into julienne strips
- 2 tbsps. vegetable oil
- 4 peeled fresh ginger slices, each about the size of a quarter
- Kosher salt
- 4 ounces (113 g) snow peas, thinly sliced on the diagonal
- 2 tbsps. hoisin sauce
- 1 tbsp. water

### DIRECTIONS:

1. Before getting started, be sure to remove the Crisper Tray from the pot.
2. In a bowl, stir together the rice wine, light soy, and chili paste. Add the pork and toss to coat. Set aside to marinate for 10 minutes.
3. Flip the SmartSwitch to AIRFRY/STOVETOP. Select SEAR/SAUTÉ, choose "4". Press START/STOP to begin cooking.
4. Pour in the vegetable oil in the pot. Season the oil by adding the ginger and a pinch of salt. Allow the ginger to sizzle in the oil for about 30 seconds, swirling gently.
5. Add the pork and marinade and sauté for 2 to 3 minutes, until no longer pink. Add the snow peas and sauté for about 1 minute, until tender and translucent. Stir in the hoisin sauce and water to loosen the sauce. Continue to toss and flip for 30 seconds, or until the sauce is heated through and the pork and snow peas are coated.
6. Transfer to a platter and serve hot.

## ROAST PORK WITH RED CABBAGE (SLOW COOK)

Prep Time: 20 minutes, Cook Time: 9 hours, Serves: 6 to 8

### INGREDIENTS:

- 1 (3-pound / 1.4-kg) pork loin roast
- 1 large head red cabbage, chopped
- 2 medium pears, peeled and chopped
- 2 red onions, chopped
- 1 cup chicken stock
- ¼ cup apple cider vinegar
- 4 garlic cloves, minced
- 3 tbsps. honey
- 1 tsp. dried thyme leaves
- ½ tsp. salt

### DIRECTIONS:

1. Before getting started, be sure to remove the crisper tray.
2. Mix the cabbage, onions, pears, and garlic in the bottom of the pot.
3. In a small bowl, mix the vinegar, honey, chicken stock, thyme, and salt, and pour the mixture into the pot.
4. Place the pork on top, nestling the meat into the vegetables.
5. Close the lid and flip the SmartSwitch to AIRFRY/STOVETOP. Select SLOW COOK, set temperature to "Lo", and set time to 9 hours. Press START/STOP to begin cooking, until the pork is soft.
6. Enjoy!

## SAVORY POT ROAST AND POTATO (SLOW COOK)

Prep Time: 13 minutes, Cook Time: 9 hours, Serves: 10

### INGREDIENTS:

- 1 (3-pound / 1.4-kg) grass-fed chuck shoulder roast or tri-tip roast
- 8 Yukon Gold potatoes, cut into chunks
- 4 large carrots, peeled and cut into chunks
- 2 onions, chopped
- 1 leek, sliced
- 1 cup beef stock
- 8 garlic cloves, sliced
- 1 tsp. dried marjoram
- ½ tsp. salt
- ¼ tsp. freshly ground black pepper

### DIRECTIONS:

1. Before getting started, be sure to remove the crisper tray.
2. Mix the potatoes, carrots, onions, leek, and garlic in the bottom of the pot.
3. Put the beef on top of the vegetables and scatter with the marjoram, salt, and pepper.
4. Add the beef stock into the pot.
5. Close the lid and flip the SmartSwitch to AIRFRY/STOVETOP. Select SLOW COOK, set temperature to "Lo", and set time to 9 hours. Press START/STOP to begin cooking, until the beef is very soft.
6. Serve the beef with the vegetables.

## CRISPY SIRLOIN STEAK (AIR FRY)

Prep Time: 15 minutes, Cook Time: 13 minutes, Serves: 2

### INGREDIENTS:

- cooking spray
- 1 cup white flour
- 2 eggs
- 1 cup panko breadcrumbs
- 2 (6-ounces) sirloin steaks, pounded
- 1 tsp. garlic powder
- 1 tsp. onion powder
- Salt and black pepper, to taste

### DIRECTIONS:

1. Push in the legs on the Crisper Tray, then place the tray in the bottom of the pot. Spray the tray with cooking spray.
2. Place the flour in a shallow bowl and whisk eggs in a second dish.
3. Mix the panko breadcrumbs and spices in a third bowl.
4. Rub the steak with flour, dip into the eggs and coat with breadcrumb mixture.
5. Close the lid and flip the SmartSwitch to AIRFRY/STOVETOP. Select AIRFRY, set temperature to 375°F, and set time to 18 minutes (unit will need to preheat for 5 minutes, so set an external timer if desired). Press START/STOP to begin cooking.
6. When the unit is preheated and the time reaches 13 minutes, place the steaks on the tray. Close the lid to begin cooking.
7. After 7 minutes, open the lid and flip the steak with silicone-tipped tongs to ensure even cooking. Close the lid to continue cooking.
8. Dish out the steak and cut into desired size slices to serve.

## ROASTED LAMB (BAKE&ROAST)

Prep Time: 15 minutes, Cook Time: 40 minutes, Serves: 4

### INGREDIENTS:

- cooking spray
- 2½ pounds half lamb leg roast, slits carved
- 2 garlic cloves, sliced into smaller slithers
- 1 tbsp. dried rosemary
- 1 tbsp. olive oil
- Cracked Himalayan rock salt and cracked peppercorns, to taste

### DIRECTIONS:

1. Push in the legs on the Crisper Tray, then place the tray in the bottom of the pot. Spray the tray with cooking spray.
2. Insert the garlic slithers in the slits and brush with rosemary, oil, salt, and black pepper.
3. Close the lid and flip the SmartSwitch to AIRFRY/STOVETOP. Select BAKE & ROAST, set temperature to 400°F, and set time to 45 minutes (unit will need to preheat for 5 minutes, so set an external timer if desired). Press START/STOP to begin cooking.
4. When the unit is preheated and the time reaches 40 minutes, place the lamb on the tray. Close the lid to begin cooking.
5. Dish out the lamb chops and serve hot.

## LAMB WITH POTATOES (BAKE&ROAST)

Prep Time: 20 minutes, Cook Time: 30 minutes, Serves: 2

### INGREDIENTS:

- cooking spray
- ½ pound lamb meat
- 2 small potatoes, peeled and halved
- ½ small onion, peeled and halved
- 1 garlic clove, crushed
- ½ tbsp. dried rosemary, crushed
- 1 tsp. olive oil

### DIRECTIONS:

1. Push in the legs on the Crisper Tray, then place the tray in the bottom of the pot. Spray the tray with cooking spray.
2. Rub the lamb evenly with garlic and rosemary.
3. Close the lid and flip the SmartSwitch to AIRFRY/STOVETOP. Select BAKE & ROAST, set temperature to 375°F, and set time to 35 minutes (unit will need to preheat for 5 minutes, so set an external timer if desired). Press START/STOP to begin cooking.
4. When the unit is preheated and the time reaches 30 minutes, place the lamb on the tray. Close the lid to begin cooking. Meanwhile, microwave the potatoes for about 4 minutes.
5. Dish out the potatoes in a large bowl and stir in the olive oil and onions.
6. With 15 minutes remaining, open the lid and flip the lamb with silicone-tipped tongs to ensure even cooking. Close the lid to continue cooking.
7. Dish out in a bowl.

## SMOKED BEEF (BAKE&ROAST)

Prep Time: 10 minutes, Cook Time: 20 minutes, Serves: 8

### INGREDIENTS:

- cooking spray
- 2 pounds (907 g) roast beef, at room temperature
- 2 tbsps. extra-virgin olive oil
- 1 tsp. sea salt flakes
- 1 tsp. ground black pepper
- 1 tsp. smoked paprika
- Few dashes of liquid smoke
- 2 jalapeño peppers, thinly sliced

### DIRECTIONS:

1. Push in the legs on the Crisper Tray, then place the tray in the bottom of the pot. Spray the tray with cooking spray.
2. With kitchen towels, pat the beef dry.
3. Massage the extra-virgin olive oil, salt, black pepper, and paprika into the meat. Cover with liquid smoke.
4. Close the lid and flip the SmartSwitch to AIRFRY/STOVETOP. Select BAKE & ROAST, set temperature to 390°F, and set time to 25 minutes (unit will need to preheat for 5 minutes, so set an external timer if desired). Press START/STOP to begin cooking.
5. When the unit is preheated and the time reaches 20 minutes, place the beef on the tray. Close the lid to begin cooking.
6. After 10 minutes, open the lid and flip the roast with silicone-tipped tongs to ensure even cooking. Close the lid to continue cooking.
7. When cooked through, serve topped with sliced jalapeños.

## ROSEMARY RIBEYE STEAKS (BAKE&ROAST)

Prep Time: 10 minutes, Cook Time: 15 minutes, Serves: 2

### INGREDIENTS:

- cooking spray
- ¼ cup butter
- 1 clove garlic, minced
- Salt and ground black pepper, to taste
- 1½ tbsps. balsamic vinegar
- ¼ cup rosemary, chopped
- 2 ribeye steaks

### DIRECTIONS:

1. Push in the legs on the Crisper Tray, then place the tray in the bottom of the pot. Spray the tray with cooking spray.
2. Melt the butter in a skillet over medium heat. Add the garlic and fry until fragrant.
3. Remove the skillet from the heat and add the salt, pepper, and vinegar. Allow it to cool.
4. Add the rosemary, then pour the mixture into a Ziploc bag.
5. Put the ribeye steaks in the bag and shake well, coating the meat well. Refrigerate for an hour, then allow to sit for a further twenty minutes.
6. Close the lid and flip the SmartSwitch to AIRFRY/STOVETOP. Select BAKE & ROAST, set temperature to 390°F, and set time to 20 minutes (unit will need to preheat for 5 minutes, so set an external timer if desired). Press START/STOP to begin cooking.
7. When the unit is preheated and the time reaches 15 minutes, place the ribeyes on the tray. Close the lid to begin cooking.
8. After 8 minutes, open the lid and slip the steaks with silicone-tipped tongs to ensure even cooking. Close the lid to continue cooking.
9. Take care when transferring the steaks and plate up.

## MEXICAN PORK CHOPS (BAKE&ROAST)

Prep Time: 5 minutes, Cook Time: 17 minutes, Serves: 2

### INGREDIENTS:

- cooking spray
- ¼ tsp. dried oregano
- 1½ tsps. taco seasoning mix
- 2 (4-ounce / 113-g) boneless pork chops
- 2 tbsps. unsalted butter, divided

### DIRECTIONS:

1. Push in the legs on the Crisper Tray, then place the tray in the bottom of the pot. Spray the tray with cooking spray.
2. Combine the dried oregano and taco seasoning in a small bowl and rub the mixture into the pork chops. Brush the chops with 1 tbsp. butter.
3. Close the lid and flip the SmartSwitch to AIRFRY/STOVETOP. Select BAKE & ROAST, set temperature to 375°F, and set time to 22 minutes (unit will need to preheat for 5 minutes, so set an external timer if desired). Press START/STOP to begin cooking.
4. When the unit is preheated and the time reaches 17 minutes, place the chops on the tray. Close the lid to begin cooking.
5. After 10 minutes, open the lid and flip the chops with silicone-tipped tongs to ensure even cooking. Close the lid to continue cooking.
6. Serve with a garnish of remaining butter.

## CITRUS PORK LOIN ROAST (BAKE&ROAST)

Prep Time: 10 minutes, Cook Time: 35 minutes, Serves: 8

### INGREDIENTS:

- 1 tbsp. lime juice
- 1 tbsp. orange marmalade
- 1 tsp. coarse brown mustard
- 1 tsp. curry powder
- 1 tsp. dried lemongrass
- 2 pound (907 g) boneless pork loin roast
- Salt and ground black pepper, to taste
- Cooking spray

### DIRECTIONS:

1. Push in the legs on the Crisper Tray, then place the tray in the bottom of the pot. Spray the tray with cooking spray.
2. Mix the lime juice, marmalade, mustard, curry powder, and lemongrass.
3. Rub mixture all over the surface of the pork loin. Season with salt and pepper.
4. Close the lid and flip the SmartSwitch to AIRFRY/STOVETOP. Select BAKE & ROAST, set temperature to 375°F, and set time to 40 minutes (unit will need to preheat for 5 minutes, so set an external timer if desired). Press START/STOP to begin cooking.
5. When the unit is preheated and the time reaches 35 minutes, place the pork roast diagonally on the tray. Close the lid to begin cooking.
6. After 20 minutes, open the lid and flip the pork roast with silicone-tipped tongs to ensure even cooking. Close the lid to continue cooking, until the internal temperature reaches at least 145ºF (63ºC).
7. Wrap roast in foil and let rest for 10 minutes before slicing.

## MOIST STUFFED PORK ROLL (BAKE&ROAST)

Prep Time: 20 minutes, Cook Time: 15 minutes, Serves: 4

### INGREDIENTS:

- cooking spray
- 1 scallion, chopped
- ¼ cup sun-dried tomatoes, chopped finely
- 2 tbsps. fresh parsley, chopped
- 4 (6-ounce) pork cutlets, pounded slightly
- Salt and black pepper, to taste
- 2 tsps. paprika
- ½ tbsp. olive oil

### DIRECTIONS:

1. Push in the legs on the Crisper Tray, then place the tray in the bottom of the pot. Spray the tray with cooking spray.
2. Mix scallion, tomatoes, parsley, salt and black pepper in a large bowl.
3. Coat the cutlets with tomato mixture and roll each cutlet.
4. Secure the cutlets with cocktail sticks and rub with paprika, salt and black pepper. Coat evenly with oil.
5. Close the lid and flip the SmartSwitch to AIRFRY/STOVETOP. Select BAKE & ROAST, set temperature to 375°F, and set time to 20 minutes (unit will need to preheat for 5 minutes, so set an external timer if desired). Press START/STOP to begin cooking.
6. When the unit is preheated and the time reaches 15 minutes, place the cutlets on the tray. Close the lid to begin cooking.
7. After 8 minutes, open the lid and flip the cutlets with silicone-tipped tongs to ensure even cooking. Close the lid to continue cooking.
8. Dish out to serve hot.

## BEEF AND LENTILS RICE MEAL (SPEEDI MEALS)

Prep: 20 minutes, Total Cook Time: 22 minutes, Steam: approx. 10 minutes, Cook: 12 minutes, Serves: 2

### INGREDIENTS:

- LEVEL 1 (BOTTOM OF POT)
- 1 tbsp. olive oil
- ½ cup chopped onion
- 2 cloves garlic, minced
- 3 cups water
- 1 cup brown lentils
- 1 cup brown rice
- 2-inch sprig fresh rosemary

- 1 tbsp. dried marjoram
- LEVEL 2 (TRAY)
- 1 tbsp. olive oil
- 2 beef steaks
- ½ tsp. garlic salt
- 1 garlic clove, crushed
- 2 tbsps. lemon juice

### DIRECTIONS:

1. Place all Level 1 ingredients in the pot and stir to combine.
2. Pull out the legs on the Crisper Tray, then place the tray in the elevated position in the pot.
3. Mix the beef steaks with the remaining ingredients. Place the beef steaks on top of the tray.
4. Close the lid and flip the SmartSwitch to RAPID COOKER.
5. Select SPEEDI MEALS, set temperature to 350°F, and set time to 12 minutes. Press START/STOP to begin cooking (the unit will steam for approx. 10 minutes before crisping).
6. When cooking is complete, remove the beef steaks from the tray. Then use silicone-tipped tongs to grab the center handle and remove the tray from the unit. Transfer the lentil and rice to a bowl, then top with the beef steaks.

## CHINESE PORK AND MUSHROOM PASTA (SPEEDI MEALS)

Prep: 20 minutes, Total Cook Time: 24 minutes, Steam: approx. 10 minutes, Cook: 14 minutes, Serves: 4

### INGREDIENTS:

- LEVEL 1 (BOTTOM OF POT)
- 1 tbsp. oil
- 8 ounces (227 g) mushrooms, minced
- ½ tsp. kosher salt
- ½ tsp. black ground pepper
- 8 ounces (227 g) uncooked spaghetti pasta
- 2 cups water
- ½ cup pesto

- ⅓ cup grated Parmesan cheese
- LEVEL 2 (TRAY)
- 4 tbsps. coconut oil
- 4 garlic cloves, minced
- 1 tbsp. fresh ginger
- 4 boneless pork chops
- 2 tbsps. soy sauce
- Salt and pepper, to taste

### DIRECTIONS:

1. Place all Level 1 ingredients in the pot and stir to combine.
2. Pull out the legs on the Crisper Tray, then place the tray in the elevated position in the pot.
3. In a large bowl, mix the pork chops with the remaining ingredients. Marinade for 5 minutes. Place the pork chops on top of the tray.
4. Close the lid and flip the SmartSwitch to RAPID COOKER.
5. Select SPEEDI MEALS, set temperature to 375°F, and set time to 14 minutes. Press START/STOP to begin cooking (the unit will steam for approx. 10 minutes before crisping).
6. When cooking is complete, remove the pork chops from the tray. Then use silicone-tipped tongs to grab the center handle and remove the tray from the unit. Transfer the mushroom pasta to a bowl, then top with the pork chops.
7. Serve hot.

# PINE NUT PORK AND OLIVE PASTA (SPEEDI MEALS)

Prep: 25 minutes, Total Cook Time: 30-35 minutes, Steam: approx. 10-15 minutes, Cook: 20 minutes, Serves: 4

## INGREDIENTS:

- LEVEL 1 (BOTTOM OF POT)
- 3 cloves garlic, minced
- 4 cups pasta such as penne or fusilli (short pasta)
- 4 cups pasta sauce (homemade or store-bought)
- 4 cups water
- 1 tbsp. of capers
- ½ cup Kalamata olives, sliced
- ¼ tsp. crushed red pepper flakes
- Salt and pepper, to taste
- LEVEL 2 (TRAY)
- 1½ lbs. pork tenderloin
- 1 tsp. sea salt
- 1 tbsp. extra virgin olive oil
- 1 medium onion, finely sliced
- ½ cup pine nuts
- 1 cup pesto sauce

## DIRECTIONS:

1. Place all Level 1 ingredients in the pot and stir to combine.
2. Pull out the legs on the Crisper Tray, then place the tray in the elevated position in the pot.
3. In a large bowl, mix the pork tenderloin with the remaining ingredients. Place the pork tenderloin on top of the tray.
4. Close the lid and flip the SmartSwitch to RAPID COOKER.
5. Select SPEEDI MEALS, set temperature to 375°F, and set time to 20 minutes. Press START/STOP to begin cooking (the unit will steam for approx. 10 to 15 minutes before crisping).
6. When cooking is complete, remove the pork tenderloin from the tray. Then use silicone-tipped tongs to grab the center handle and remove the tray from the unit. Transfer the pasta mixture to a bowl, then top with the pork tenderloin.
7. Serve hot.

# CHAPTER 7
# SNACK AND DESSERT

## AIR FRIED OLIVES (AIR FRY)

Prep Time: 5 minutes, Cook Time: 8 minutes, Serves: 4

### INGREDIENTS:

- 1 (5½-ounce / 156-g) jar pitted green olives
- ½ cup all-purpose flour
- Salt and pepper, to taste
- ½ cup bread crumbs
- 1 egg
- Cooking spray

### DIRECTIONS:

1. Push in the legs on the Crisper Tray, then place the tray in the bottom of the pot. Spray the tray with cooking spray.
2. Remove the olives from the jar and dry thoroughly with paper towels.
3. In a small bowl, combine the flour with salt and pepper to taste. Place the bread crumbs in another small bowl. In a third small bowl, beat the egg.
4. Dip the olives in the flour, then the egg, and then the bread crumbs.
5. Close the lid and flip the SmartSwitch to AIRFRY/STOVETOP. Select AIRFRY, set temperature to 400°F, and set time to 13 minutes (unit will need to preheat for 5 minutes, so set an external timer if desired). Press START/STOP to begin cooking.
6. When the unit is preheated and the time reaches 8 minutes, place the breaded olives on the tray. Spray the olives with cooking spray. Close the lid to begin cooking.
7. With 2 minutes remaining, open the lid and flip the olives with silicone-tipped tongs to ensure even cooking. Close the lid to continue cooking.
8. Cool before serving.

## BREADED ARTICHOKE HEARTS (AIR FRY)

Prep Time: 5 minutes, Cook Time: 8 minutes, Serves: 14

### INGREDIENTS:

- 14 whole artichoke hearts, packed in water
- 1 egg
- ½ cup all-purpose flour
- ⅓ cup panko bread crumbs
- 1 tsp. Italian seasoning
- Cooking spray

### DIRECTIONS:

1. Push in the legs on the Crisper Tray, then place the tray in the bottom of the pot. Spray the tray with cooking spray.
2. Squeeze excess water from the artichoke hearts and place them on paper towels to dry.
3. In a small bowl, beat the egg. In another small bowl, place the flour. In a third small bowl, combine the bread crumbs and Italian seasoning, and stir.
4. Dip the artichoke hearts in the flour, then the egg, and then the bread crumb mixture.
5. Close the lid and flip the SmartSwitch to AIRFRY/STOVETOP. Select AIRFRY, set temperature to 390°F, and set time to 13 minutes (unit will need to preheat for 5 minutes, so set an external timer if desired). Press START/STOP to begin cooking.
6. When the unit is preheated and the time reaches 8 minutes, place the breaded artichoke hearts on the tray. Close the lid to begin cooking.
7. After 4 minutes, open the lid and flip the artichoke hearts with silicone-tipped tongs to ensure even cooking. Close the lid to continue cooking, until the artichoke hearts have browned and are crisp.
8. Let cool for 5 minutes before serving.

# TORTILLA CHIPS (AIR FRY)

Prep Time: 5 minutes, Cook Time: 5 minutes, Serves: 2

### INGREDIENTS:

- cooking spray
- 8 corn tortillas
- 1 tbsp. olive oil
- Salt, to taste

### DIRECTIONS:

1. Push in the legs on the Crisper Tray, then place the tray in the bottom of the pot. Spray the tray with cooking spray.
2. Slice the corn tortillas into triangles. Coat with a light brushing of olive oil.
3. Close the lid and flip the SmartSwitch to AIRFRY/STOVETOP. Select AIRFRY, set temperature to 390°F, and set time to 10 minutes (unit will need to preheat for 5 minutes, so set an external timer if desired). Press START/STOP to begin cooking.
4. When the unit is preheated and the time reaches 5 minutes, place the tortilla pieces on the tray. Close the lid to begin cooking.
5. Season with salt before serving.

# MOZZARELLA ARANCINI (AIR FRY)

Prep Time: 5 minutes, Cook Time: 10 minutes, Makes: 16 arancini

### INGREDIENTS:

- 2 cups cooked rice, cooled
- 2 eggs, beaten
- 1½ cups panko bread crumbs, divided
- ½ cup grated Parmesan cheese
- 2 tbsps. minced fresh basil
- 16 ¾-inch cubes Mozzarella cheese
- 2 tbsps. olive oil

### DIRECTIONS:

1. Push in the legs on the Crisper Tray, then place the tray in the bottom of the pot. Spray the tray with cooking spray.
2. In a medium bowl, combine the rice, eggs, ½ cup of the bread crumbs, Parmesan cheese, and basil. Form this mixture into 16 1½-inch balls.
3. Poke a hole in each of the balls with your finger and insert a Mozzarella cube. Form the rice mixture firmly around the cheese.
4. On a shallow plate, combine the remaining 1 cup of the bread crumbs with the olive oil and mix well. Roll the rice balls in the bread crumbs to coat.
5. Close the lid and flip the SmartSwitch to AIRFRY/STOVETOP. Select AIRFRY, set temperature to 400°F, and set time to 15 minutes (unit will need to preheat for 5 minutes, so set an external timer if desired). Press START/STOP to begin cooking.
6. When the unit is preheated and the time reaches 10 minutes, place the arancini on the tray (you may need work in batches). Close the lid to begin cooking, until golden brown.
7. When the time is up, serve hot.

# CHEESY HASH BROWN BRUSCHETTA (AIR FRY)

Prep Time: 5 minutes, Cook Time: 12 minutes, Serves: 4

## INGREDIENTS:

- cooking spray
- 4 frozen hash brown patties
- 1 tbsp. olive oil
- ⅓ cup chopped cherry tomatoes
- 3 tbsps. diced fresh Mozzarella
- 2 tbsps. grated Parmesan cheese
- 1 tbsp. balsamic vinegar
- 1 tbsp. minced fresh basil

## DIRECTIONS:

1. Push in the legs on the Crisper Tray, then place the tray in the bottom of the pot. Spray the tray with cooking spray.
2. Close the lid and flip the SmartSwitch to AIRFRY/STOVETOP. Select AIRFRY, set temperature to 390°F, and set time to 17 minutes (unit will need to preheat for 5 minutes, so set an external timer if desired). Press START/STOP to begin cooking.
3. When the unit is preheated and the time reaches 12 minutes, place the hash brown patties on the tray. Close the lid to begin cooking.
4. Meanwhile, combine the olive oil, tomatoes, Mozzarella, Parmesan, vinegar, and basil in a small bowl.
5. After 6 minutes, open the lid and flip once with silicone-tipped tongs to ensure even cooking. Close the lid to continue cooking.
6. When cooking is complete, carefully transfer into a serving plate. Top with the tomato mixture and serve.

# SWEET BACON TATER TOTS (AIR FRY)

Prep Time: 5 minutes, Cook Time: 17 minutes, Serves: 4

## INGREDIENTS:

- cooking spray
- 24 frozen tater tots
- 6 slices cooked bacon
- 2 tbsps. maple syrup
- 1 cup shredded Cheddar cheese

## DIRECTIONS:

1. Push in the legs on the Crisper Tray, then place the tray in the bottom of the pot. Spray the tray with cooking spray.
2. Close the lid and flip the SmartSwitch to AIRFRY/STOVETOP. Select AIRFRY, set temperature to 400°F, and set time to 22 minutes (unit will need to preheat for 5 minutes, so set an external timer if desired). Press START/STOP to begin cooking.
3. When the unit is preheated and the time reaches 17 minutes, place the tater tots on the tray. Close the lid to begin cooking. Meanwhile, cut the bacon into 1-inch pieces.
4. After 10 minutes, open the lid and flip the tater tots with silicone-tipped tongs to ensure even cooking. Top with the bacon and drizzle with the maple syrup. Close the lid to continue cooking.
5. With 2 minutes remaining, open the lid and top with the cheese. Close the lid to continue cooking, until the cheese is melted.
6. Serve hot.

## CRISPY BREADED BEEF CUBES (BAKE&ROAST)

Prep Time: 10 minutes, Cook Time: 12 minutes, Serves: 4

### INGREDIENTS:

- cooking spray
- 1 pound (454 g) sirloin tip, cut into 1-inch cubes
- 1 cup cheese pasta sauce
- 1½ cups soft bread crumbs
- 2 tbsps. olive oil
- ½ tsp. dried marjoram

### DIRECTIONS:

1. Push in the legs on the Crisper Tray, then place the tray in the bottom of the pot. Spray the tray with cooking spray.
2. Toss the beef with the pasta sauce to coat evenly in a medium bowl.
3. In a shallow bowl, Mix the bread crumbs, oil, and marjoram, and mix well. Dip the beef cubes, one at a time, into the bread crumb mixture to coat thoroughly.
4. Close the lid and flip the SmartSwitch to AIRFRY/STOVETOP. Select BAK&ROAST, set temperature to 350°F, and set time to 17 minutes (unit will need to preheat for 5 minutes, so set an external timer if desired). Press START/STOP to begin cooking.
5. When the unit is preheated and the time reaches 12 minutes, place the beef cubes on the tray. Close the lid to begin cooking.
6. After 5 minutes, open the lid and toss the beef cubes with silicone-tipped tongs to ensure even cooking. Close the lid to continue cooking, until the beef is at least 145ºF and the outside is crisp and brown.
7. Serve hot.

## LEMONY BLACKBERRY CRISP (BAKE&ROAST)

Prep Time: 5 minutes, Cook Time: 15 minutes, Serves: 1

### INGREDIENTS:

- cooking spray
- 2 tbsps. lemon juice
- ⅓ cup powdered erythritol
- ¼ tsp. xantham gum
- 2 cup blackberries
- 1 cup crunchy granola

### DIRECTIONS:

1. Push in the legs on the Crisper Tray, then place the tray in the bottom of the pot. Spray a 8-inch round baking pan with cooking spray.
2. In a bowl, combine the lemon juice, erythritol, xantham gum, and blackberries. Transfer to the baking pan and cover with aluminum foil.
3. Close the lid and flip the SmartSwitch to AIRFRY/STOVETOP. Select BAKE & ROAST, set temperature to 350°F, and set time to 20 minutes (unit will need to preheat for 5 minutes, so set an external timer if desired). Press START/STOP to begin cooking.
4. When the unit is preheated and the time reaches 15 minutes, place the pan on the tray. Close the lid to begin cooking.
5. With 3 minutes remaining, open the lid. Give the blackberries a stir and top with the granola. Close the lid and reduce the temperature to 320ºF to continue cooking.
6. Serve once the granola has turned brown and enjoy.

# RICH CHOCOLATE COOKIE (BAKE&ROAST)

Prep Time: 10 minutes, Cook Time: 9 minutes, Serves: 4

## INGREDIENTS:

- Nonstick baking spray with flour
- 3 tbsps. softened butter
- ⅓ cup plus 1 tbsp. brown sugar
- 1 egg yolk
- ½ cup flour
- 2 tbsps. ground white chocolate
- ¼ tsp. baking soda
- ½ tsp. vanilla
- ¾ cup chocolate chips

## DIRECTIONS:

1. Push in the legs on the Crisper Tray, then place the tray in the bottom of the pot. In a medium bowl, beat the butter and brown sugar together until fluffy. Stir in the egg yolk.
2. Add the flour, white chocolate, baking soda, and vanilla, and mix well. Stir in the chocolate chips.
3. Line a baking pan with parchment paper. Spray the parchment paper with nonstick baking spray with flour.
4. Spread the batter into the prepared pan, leaving a ½-inch border on all sides.
5. Close the lid and flip the SmartSwitch to AIRFRY/STOVETOP. Select BAKE & ROAST, set temperature to 350°F, and set time to 14 minutes (unit will need to preheat for 5 minutes, so set an external timer if desired). Press START/STOP to begin cooking.
6. When the unit is preheated and the time reaches 9 minutes, place the pan on the tray. Close the lid to begin cooking, until the cookie is light brown and just barely set.
7. Remove the pan and let cool for 10 minutes. Remove the cookie from the pan, remove the parchment paper, and let cool on a wire rack.
8. Serve immediately.

# CINNAMON AND PECAN PIE (BAKE&ROAST)

Prep Time: 10 minutes, Cook Time: 30 minutes, Serves: 4

## INGREDIENTS:

- cooking spray
- 1 pie dough
- ½ tsps. cinnamon
- ¾ tsp. vanilla extract
- 2 eggs
- ¾ cup maple syrup
- ⅛ tsp. nutmeg
- 3 tbsps. melted butter, divided
- 2 tbsps. sugar
- ½ cup chopped pecans

## DIRECTIONS:

1. Push in the legs on the Crisper Tray, then place the tray in the bottom of the pot. Spray a pie pan with cooking spray.
2. In a small bowl, coat the pecans in 1 tbsp. of melted butter.
3. Close the lid and flip the SmartSwitch to AIRFRY/STOVETOP. Select BAKE & ROAST, set temperature to 375°F, and set time to 35 minutes (unit will need to preheat for 5 minutes, so set an external timer if desired). Press START/STOP to begin cooking.
4. When the unit is preheated and the time reaches 30 minutes, place the pecans on the tray. Close the lid to begin cooking.
5. With 20 minutes remaining, open the lid. Put the pie dough in the greased pie pan and add the pecans on top. In a bowl, mix the rest of the ingredients. Pour this over the pecans. Transfer the pie pan on the tray. Close the lid to continue cooking.
6. Serve immediately.

## PEPPERY CHICKEN MEATBALLS (STEAM&CRISP)

Prep: 5 minutes, Total Cook Time: 20-22 minutes, Steam: approx. 4 minutes, Cook: 16-18 minutes, Makes: 16 meatballs

### INGREDIENTS:

- 1 cup water, for steaming
- 2 tsps. olive oil
- ¼ cup minced onion
- ¼ cup minced red bell pepper
- 2 vanilla wafers, crushed
- 1 egg white
- ½ tsp. dried thyme
- ½ pound (227 g) ground chicken breast

### DIRECTIONS:

1. Pour ½ cup water into the pot. Push in the legs on the Crisper Tray, then place the tray in the bottom position in the pot.
2. In a skillet over medium heat, add the olive oil, onion, and red bell pepper. Sauté for 3 to 5 minutes, until the vegetables are tender.
3. In a medium bowl, mix the cooked vegetables, crushed wafers, egg white, and thyme until well combined.
4. Mix in the chicken, gently but thoroughly, until everything is combined. Form the mixture into 16 meatballs. Place the meatballs on the tray.
5. Close the lid and flip the SmartSwitch to Rapid Cooker. Select STEAM & CRISP, set temperature to 350°F, and set time to 13 minutes. Press START/STOP to begin cooking (the unit will steam for approx. 4 minutes before crisping).
6. With 6 minutes remaining, open the lid and flip the side with tongs. Close the lid to continue cooking.
7. Serve immediately.

## VEGGIE SALMON NACHOS (STEAM&CRISP)

Prep: 10 minutes, Total Cook Time: 11 minutes, Steam: approx. 4 minutes, Cook: 7 minutes, Serves: 6

### INGREDIENTS:

- ¼ cup water, for steaming
- 2 ounces (57 g) baked no-salt corn tortilla chips
- 1 (5-ounce / 142-g) baked salmon fillet, flaked
- ½ cup canned low-sodium black beans, rinsed and drained
- 1 red bell pepper, chopped
- ½ cup grated carrot
- 1 jalapeño pepper, minced
- ⅓ cup shredded low-sodium low-fat Swiss cheese
- 1 tomato, chopped

### DIRECTIONS:

1. Pour ¼ cup water into the pot. Pull out the legs on the Crisper Tray, then place the tray in the elevated position in the pot.
2. Layer the tortilla chips on the tray. Top with the salmon, black beans, red bell pepper, carrot, jalapeño, and Swiss cheese.
3. Close the lid and flip the SmartSwitch to Rapid Cooker. Select STEAM & CRISP, set temperature to 450°F, and set time to 7 minutes. Press START/STOP to begin cooking (the unit will steam for approx. 4 minutes before crisping).
4. When cooking is complete, top with the tomato and serve.

# CHOCOLATE MOLTEN CAKE (STEAM&BAKE)

Prep: 5 minutes, Total Cook Time: 25 minutes, Steam: approx. 15 minutes, Cook: 10 minutes, Serves: 4

## INGREDIENTS:

- 1 cup water, for steaming
- 2 eggs
- 3.5 ounces (99 g) butter, melted
- 3.5 ounces (99 g) chocolate, melted
- 3½ tbsps. sugar
- 1½ tbsps. flour

## DIRECTIONS:

1. Pour 1 cup water into the pot. Push in the legs on the Crisper Tray, then place the tray in the bottom position in the pot. Grease four ramekins lightly with a little butter.
2. Rigorously mix the eggs, butter, and sugar before stirring in the melted chocolate. Gently fold in the flour. Scoop an equal amount of the mixture into each ramekin. Put them on the tray.
3. Close the lid and flip the SmartSwitch to Rapid Cooker. Select STEAM & BAKE, set temperature to 375°F, and set time to 10 minutes. Press START/STOP to begin cooking (the unit will steam for approx. 15 minutes before baking).
4. When cooking is complete, transfer the ramekins upside-down on plates and let the cakes fall out. Serve warm.

# BANANA AND WALNUT CAKE (STEAM&BAKE)

Prep: 10 minutes, Total Cook Time: 45 minutes, Steam: approx. 20 minutes, Cook: 25 minutes, Serves: 6

## INGREDIENTS:

- 2 cups water, for steaming
- cooking spray
- 1 pound (454 g) bananas, mashed
- 8 ounces (227 g) flour
- 6 ounces (170 g) sugar
- 3.5 ounces (99 g) walnuts, chopped
- 2.5 ounces (71 g) butter, melted
- 2 eggs, lightly beaten
- ¼ tsp. baking soda

## DIRECTIONS:

1. Pour 2 cups water into the pot. Push in the legs on the Crisper Tray, then place the tray in the bottom position in the pot. Spray a 8-inch round baking pan with cooking spray.
2. In a bowl, combine the sugar, butter, egg, flour, and baking soda with a whisk. Stir in the bananas and walnuts.
3. Transfer the mixture to the greased baking pan. Put the pan on the tray.
4. Close the lid and flip the SmartSwitch to Rapid Cooker. Select STEAM & BAKE, set temperature to 350°F, and set time to 25 minutes. Press START/STOP to begin cooking (the unit will steam for approx. 20 minutes before baking).
5. With 15 minutes remaining, reduce the temperature to 330ºF. Continue cooking until the cake is golden down.
6. Serve hot.

## ORANGE CAKE (STEAM&BAKE)

Prep: 10 minutes, Total Cook Time: 37 minutes, Steam: approx. 20 minutes, Cook: 17 minutes, Serves: 8

### INGREDIENTS:

- 2 cups water, for steaming
- Nonstick baking spray with flour
- 1¼ cups all-purpose flour
- ⅓ cup yellow cornmeal
- ¾ cup white sugar
- 1 tsp. baking soda
- ¼ cup safflower oil
- 1¼ cups orange juice, divided
- 1 tsp. vanilla
- ¼ cup powdered sugar

### DIRECTIONS:

1. Pour 2 cups water into the pot. Push in the legs on the Crisper Tray, then place the tray in the bottom position in the pot. Spray a 8-inch round baking pan with cooking spray.
2. In a medium bowl, combine the flour, cornmeal, sugar, baking soda, safflower oil, 1 cup of the orange juice, and vanilla, and mix well.
3. Pour the batter into the baking pan and place on the tray.
4. Close the lid and flip the SmartSwitch to Rapid Cooker. Select STEAM & BAKE, set temperature to 315°F, and set time to 17 minutes. Press START/STOP to begin cooking (the unit will steam for approx. 20 minutes before baking).
5. When cooking is complete, transfer the cake on a cooling rack. Using a toothpick, make about 20 holes in the cake.
6. In a small bowl, combine remaining ¼ cup of orange juice and the powdered sugar and stir well. Drizzle this mixture over the hot cake slowly so the cake absorbs it.
7. Cool completely, then cut into wedges to serve.

## PINEAPPLE AND CHOCOLATE CAKE (STEAM&BAKE)

Prep: 10 minutes, Total Cook Time: 40 minutes, Steam: approx. 15 minutes, Cook: 25 minutes, Serves: 4

### INGREDIENTS:

- 2 cups water, for steaming
- cooking spray
- 2 cups flour
- 4 ounces (113 g) butter, melted
- ¼ cup sugar
- ½ pound (227 g) pineapple, chopped
- ½ cup pineapple juice
- 1 ounce (28 g) dark chocolate, grated
- 1 large egg
- 2 tbsps. skimmed milk

### DIRECTIONS:

1. Pour 2 cups water into the pot. Push in the legs on the Crisper Tray, then place the tray in the bottom position in the pot. Spray a cake tin with cooking spray.
2. In a bowl, combine the butter and flour to create a crumbly consistency.
3. Add the sugar, chopped pineapple, juice, and grated dark chocolate and mix well.
4. In a separate bowl, combine the egg and milk. Add this mixture to the flour mixture and stir well until a soft dough forms.
5. Pour the mixture into the cake tin and transfer on the tray.
6. Close the lid and flip the SmartSwitch to Rapid Cooker. Select STEAM & BAKE, set temperature to 350°F, and set time to 25 minutes. Press START/STOP to begin cooking (the unit will steam for approx. 15 minutes before baking).
7. When cooking is complete, serve immediately.

# BOURBON MONKEY BREAD (STEAM&BAKE)

Prep: 15 minutes, Total Cook Time: 45 minutes, Steam: approx. 25 minutes, Cook: 20 minutes, Serves: 6 to 8

## INGREDIENTS:

- 3 cups water, for steaming
- cooking spray
- 1 (16.3-ounce / 462-g) can store-bought refrigerated biscuit dough
- ¼ cup packed light brown sugar
- 1 tsp. ground cinnamon
- ½ tsp. freshly grated nutmeg
- ½ tsp. ground ginger
- ½ tsp. kosher salt
- ¼ tsp. ground allspice
- ⅛ tsp. ground cloves
- 4 tbsps. (½ stick) unsalted butter, melted
- ½ cup powdered sugar
- 2 tsps. bourbon
- 2 tbsps. chopped candied cherries
- 2 tbsps. chopped pecans

## DIRECTIONS:

1. Pour 3 cups water into the pot. Push in the legs on the Crisper Tray, then place the tray in the bottom position in the pot. Spray a 8-inch round baking pan with cooking spray.
2. Open the can and separate the biscuits, then cut each into quarters. Toss the biscuit quarters in a large bowl with the brown sugar, cinnamon, nutmeg, ginger, salt, allspice, and cloves until evenly coated. Transfer the dough pieces and any sugar left in the bowl to the baking pan and drizzle evenly with the melted butter. Put the pan on the tray.
3. Close the lid and flip the SmartSwitch to Rapid Cooker. Select STEAM & BAKE, set temperature to 315°F, and set time to 20 minutes. Press START/STOP to begin cooking (the unit will steam for approx. 25 minutes before baking).
4. When cooking is complete, transfer the pan to a wire rack and let cool completely. Unmold from the pan.
5. In a small bowl, whisk the powdered sugar and the bourbon into a smooth glaze. Drizzle the glaze over the cooled monkey bread and, while the glaze is still wet, sprinkle with the cherries and pecans to serve.

# APPENDIX 1: NINJA SPEEDI SF301 TIMETABLE

## Steam & Crisp Chart

| INGREDIENT | AMOUNT | PREPARATION | WATER | ORIENTATION | TEMP | COOK TIME |
|---|---|---|---|---|---|---|
| **VEGETABLES** | | | | | | |
| Acorn squash | 1 | Cut in half, placed face down | ½ cup | Bottom | 390°F | 15 mins |
| Beets | 2½ lbs | Cut in 1-in pieces | ½ cup | Bottom | 400°F | 30–35 mins |
| Broccoli | 1 head | Whole, stem removed | ½ cup | Bottom | 400°F | 10-15 mins |
| Brussels sprouts | 2 lbs | Cut in half, ends trimmed | ½ cup | Bottom | 450°F | 15–20 mins |
| Carrots | 1 lb | Cut in 1-in pieces | ½ cup | Bottom | 400°F | 20-25 mins |
| Cauliflower | 1 head | Whole, stems removed | ½ cup | Bottom | 425°F | 20-25 mins |
| Parsnip | 2½ lbs | Cut in 1-in pieces | ½ cup | Bottom | 400°F | 30-35 mins |
| Potatoes, russet | 2 lbs | Cut in 1-in wedges | ½ cup | Bottom | 450°F | 25–30 mins |
| | 2 lbs | Hand-cut fries, soaked 30 mins in cold water then patted dry | ½ cup | Bottom | 450°F | 30–35 mins |
| | 4 | Whole (medium), poked several times with a fork | 1 cup | Bottom | 400°F | 30–35 mins |
| | | Whole (large), poked several times with a fork | 1 cup | Bottom | 400°F | 40–48 mins |
| | 2½ lbs | Cut in 1-in pieces | ½ cup | Bottom | 450°F | 30–35 mins |
| Spaghetti squash | 1 small squash | Cut in half, deseeded, punctured with fork about 10 times | 2 cups | Bottom | 375°F | 25–30 mins |
| Sweet potatoes | 2½ lbs | Cut in 1-in pieces | ½ cup | Bottom | 450°F | 20–25 mins |
| **POULTRY** | | | | | | |
| Whole chicken | 4½–5 lbs | Trussed | 1 cup | Bottom | 400°F | 40–50 mins |
| Turkey drumstricks | 2 lbs | None | 1 cup | Bottom | 400°F | 32–38 mins |
| Turkey breast | 1 (3–5 lbs) | None | 1 cup | Bottom | 365°F | 45–55 mins |
| Chicken breasts (boneless) | 4 breasts, 6–8 oz each | Brush with oil | ½ cup | Elevated | 390°F | 15–20 mins |
| Chicken breasts (bone in, skin on) | 4 breasts, ¾–1½ lbs | Brush with oil | ½ cup | Elevated | 375°F | 20–25 mins |
| Chicken thighs (bone in) | 4 thighs, 6–10 oz each | Brush with oil | ½ cup | Elevated | 400°F | 20–25 mins |
| Chicken thighs (boneless) | 6 thighs, 4–8 oz each | Brush with oil | ½ cup | Elevated | 375°F | 15–18 mins |
| Chicken drumsticks | 2 lbs | Brush with oil | ½ cup | Elevated | 425°F | 20–25 mins |
| Hand-breaded chicken breasts | 4 breasts, 6 oz each | | ½ cup | Elevated | 385°F | 18–20 mins |
| Chicken wings | 2 lbs | | ½ cup | Bottom | 450°F | 20–25 mins |
| **PORK** | | | | | | |
| Pork tenderloins | 2 (1 lb each) | None | 1 cup | Elevated | 375°F | 25–30 mins |
| Pork loin | 1 (2 lbs) | None | 1 cup | Elevated | 365°F | 35–40 mins |
| Spiral ham, bone in | 1 (3 lbs) | None | 1 cup | Elevated | 325°F | 45–50 mins |
| Pork chops, boneless | 4 chops, 6–8 oz each | None | ½ cup | Bottom | 375°F | 15-20 mins |
| Pork chops (bone in, thick cut) | 2 chops, 10–12 oz each | | ½ cup | Bottom | 375°F | 25–30 mins |

**\*NOTE:** Crisper tray position varies, as specified in chart. Steam will take approximately 4–8 minutes to build.

# Steam & Crisp Chart

| INGREDIENT | AMOUNT | PREPARATION | WATER | ORIENTATION | TEMP | COOK TIME |
|---|---|---|---|---|---|---|
| **FISH** | | | | | | |
| Cod | 4 fillets, 6 oz each | | ½ cup | Elevated | 450°F | 9–12 mins |
| Salmon | 4 fillets, 6 oz each | | ¼ cup | Elevated | 450°F | 7–10 mins |
| Scallops | 1 lb (approx. 21 pieces) | | ¼ cup | Elevated | 400°F | 4–6 mins |
| **BEEF** | | | | | | |
| Roast beef | 2–3 lbs | None | 1 cup | Bottom | 360°F | 45 mins for medium rare |
| Tenderloin | 2–3 lbs | None | 1 cup | Bottom | 365°F | 25–30 mins for medium rare |
| **FROZEN CHICKEN** | | | | | | |
| Chicken Breasts, Boneless, Skinless | 4 breasts, 4–6 oz each | As desired | ½ cup | Elevated | 390°F | 20–25 mins |
| Chicken Thighs, Boneless, Skinless | 6 thighs, 4–8 oz each | As desired | ½ cup | Elevated | 375°F | 15–20 mins |
| Chicken Thighs, Bone-in Skin on | 4 thighs, 8–10 oz each | As desired | ½ cup | Elevated | 400°F | 20–25 mins |
| Pre-Breaded Chicken Breasts | 3–4 breasts, 10–16 oz each | As desired | ½ cup | Elevated | 375°F | 10–15 mins |
| Chicken Wings | 2 lbs | As desired | ½ cup | Bottom | 450°F | 25–30 mins |
| **FROZEN BEEF** | | | | | | |
| NY Strip Steak | 2 steaks, 10–14 oz each | 2 tbsp canola oil, salt, pepper | ¾ cup | Bottom | 400°F | 22–28 mins |
| **FROZEN FISH** | | | | | | |
| Salmon | 4 fillets, 6 oz each | | ½ cup | Elevated | 450°F | 11–15 mins |
| Shrimp | 18 shrimp, 1 lb | | ½ cup | Bottom | 450°F | 2–5 mins |
| Cod | 4 fillets, 6 oz each | | ½ cup | Elevated | 450°F | 10–15 mins |
| Lobster tails | 4 | | ½ cup | Elevated | 450°F | 5–7 mins |
| **FROZEN PORK** | | | | | | |
| Pork tenderloins | 2 (1 lb each) | None | 1½ cups | Bottom | 365°F | 30–35 mins |
| Pork loin | 1 (2 lbs) | None | None | Bottom | 360°F | 37–40 mins |
| Pork chops, boneless | 4, 6–8 oz each | | ½ cup | Elevated | 375°F | 15–20 mins |
| Pork Chops, bone-in, thick cut | 2, 10–12 oz each | | ¾ cup | Elevated | 365°F | 23–28 mins |
| Italian sausages | 6 uncooked | | ½ cup | Elevated | 375°F | 10–12 mins |
| **FROZEN PREPARED FOODS** | | | | | | |
| Dumplings/Pot stickers | 16 oz bag | | ½ cup | Bottom | 400°F | 12–16 mins |
| Ravioli | 25 oz bag | | ½ cup | Bottom | 385°F | 12–16 mins |
| Eggrolls | 10 oz pkg | | ½ cup | Bottom | 375°F | 15–20 mins |

**\*NOTE:** Crisper tray position varies, as specified in chart. Steam will take approximately 4–8 minutes to build.

# Air Fry Chart for the Crisper Tray, bottom position

| INGREDIENT | AMOUNT | PREPARATION | OIL | TEMP | COOK TIME |
|---|---|---|---|---|---|
| **VEGETABLES** | | | | | |
| Asparagus | 1 bunch | Cut in half, trim stems | 2 tsp | 390°F | 8–10 mins |
| Beets | 6 small or 4 large (about 2 lbs) | Whole | None | 390°F | 45–60 mins |
| Bell peppers | 4 peppers | Whole | None | 400°F | 25–30 mins |
| Broccoli | 1 head | Cut in 1–2-inch florets | 1 Tbsp | 390°F | 10–13 mins |
| Brussels sprouts | 1 lb | Cut in half, remove stems | 1 Tbsp | 390°F | 15–18 mins |
| Butternut squash | 1–1½ lbs | Cut in 1–2-inch pieces | 1 Tbsp | 390°F | 20–25 mins |
| Carrots | 1 lb | Peeled, cut in ½-inch pieces | 1 Tbsp | 390°F | 14–16 mins |
| Cauliflower | 1 head | Cut in 1–2-inch florets | 2 Tbsp | 390°F | 15–20 mins |
| Corn on the cob | 4 ears, cut in half | Whole, remove husks | 1 Tbsp | 390°F | 12–15 mins |
| Green beans | 1 bag (12 oz) | Trimmed | 1 Tbsp | 390°F | 7–10 mins |
| Kale (for chips) | 6 cups, packed | Tear in pieces, remove stems | None | 300°F | 8–11 mins |
| Mushrooms | 8 oz | Rinse, cut in quarters | 1 Tbsp | 390°F | 7–8 mins |
| Potatoes, russet | 1½ lbs | Cut in 1-inch wedges | 1 Tbsp | 390°F | 20–25 mins |
| | 1 lb | Hand-cut fries, thin | ½–3 Tbsp | 390°F | 20–25 mins |
| | 1 lb | Hand-cut fries, soak 30 mins in cold water then pat dry | ½–3 Tbsp | 390°F | 24–27 mins |
| | 4 whole (6–8 oz) | Pierce with fork 3 times | None | 390°F | 35–40 mins |
| Potatoes, sweet | 2 lbs | Cut in 1-inch chunks | 1 Tbsp | 390°F | 15–20 mins |
| | 4 whole (6–8 oz) | Pierce with fork 3 times | None | 390°F | 35–40 mins |
| Zucchini | 1 lb | Cut in quarters lengthwise, then cut in 1-inch pieces | 1 Tbsp | 390°F | 15–20 mins |
| **POULTRY** | | | | | |
| Chicken breasts | 2 breasts (¾–1½ lbs each) | Bone in | Brushed with oil | 375°F | 25–35 mins |
| | 2 breasts (½–¾ lb each) | Boneless | Brushed with oil | 375°F | 22–25 mins |
| Chicken thighs | 4 thighs (6–10 oz each) | Bone in | Brushed with oil | 390°F | 22–28 mins |
| | 4 thighs (4–8 oz each) | Boneless | Brushed with oil | 390°F | 18–22 mins |
| Chicken wings | 2 lbs | Drumettes & flats | 1 Tbsp | 390°F | 24–28 mins |
| Chicken, whole | 1 chicken (4–6 lbs) | Trussed | Brushed with oil | 375°F | 55–75 mins |
| Chicken drumsticks | 2 lbs | None | 1 Tbsp | 390°F | 20–22 mins |

**\*TIP** When using Air Fry, add 5 minutes to the suggested cook time for the unit to preheat before you add ingredients.

# Air Fry Chart for the Crisper Tray, bottom position

| INGREDIENT | AMOUNT | PREPARATION | OIL | TEMP | COOK TIME |
|---|---|---|---|---|---|
| **BEEF** | | | | | |
| Burgers | 4 quarter-pound patties, 80% lean | 1-inch thick | None | 375°F | 10–12 mins |
| Steaks | 2 steaks (8 oz each) | Whole | None | 390°F | 10–20 mins |
| **PORK & LAMB** | | | | | |
| Bacon | 1 strip to 1 (16 oz) package | Lay strips evenly over the plate | None | 330°F | 13–16 mins (no preheat) |
| Pork chops | 2 thick-cut, bone-in chops (10–12 oz each) | Bone in | Brushed with oil | 375°F | 15–17 mins |
| | 4 boneless chops (6–8 oz each) | Boneless | Brushed with oil | 375°F | 15–18 mins |
| Pork tenderloins | 2 tenderloins (1–1½ lbs each) | Whole | Brushed with oil | 375°F | 25–35 mins |
| Sausages | 4 sausages | Whole | None | 390°F | 8–10 mins |
| **FISH & SEAFOOD** | | | | | |
| Crab cakes | 2 cakes (6–8 oz each) | None | Brushed with oil | 350°F | 10–13 mins |
| Lobster tails | 4 tails (3–4 oz each) | Whole | None | 375°F | 7–10 mins |
| Salmon fillets | 2 fillets (4 oz each) | None | Brushed with oil | 390°F | 10–13 mins |
| Shrimp | 16 jumbo | Raw, whole, peel, keep tails on | 1 Tbsp | 390°F | 7–10 mins |
| **FROZEN FOODS** | | | | | |
| Chicken nuggets | 1 box (12 oz) | None | None | 390°F | 11–13 mins |
| Fish fillets | 1 box (6 fillets) | None | None | 390°F | 13–15 mins |
| Fish sticks | 1 box (14.8 oz) | None | None | 390°F | 9–11 mins |
| French fries | 1 lb | None | None | 360°F | 18–22 mins |
| | 2 lbs | None | None | 360°F | 28–32 mins |
| Mozzarella sticks | 1 box (11 oz) | None | None | 375°F | 6–9 mins |
| Pot stickers | 1 bag (10 count) | None | Toss with 1 tsp oil | 390°F | 11–14 mins |
| Pizza Rolls | 1 bag (20 oz, 40 count) | None | None | 390°F | 12–15 mins |
| Popcorn shrimp | 1 box (16 oz) | None | None | 390°F | 8–10 mins |
| Tater Tots | 1 lb | None | None | 360°F | 19–22 mins |

**\*TIP** When using Air Fry, add 5 minutes to the suggested cook time for the unit to preheat before you add ingredients.

# Dehydrate Chart for the Crisper Tray, bottom position

| INGREDIENT | PREPARATION | TEMP | DEHYDRATE TIME |
|---|---|---|---|
| **FRUITS & VEGETABLES** | | | |
| Apple chips | Cut in ⅛-inch slices (remove core), rinse in lemon water, pat dry | 135°F | 7–8 hrs |
| Asparagus | Cut in 1-inch pieces, blanch | 135°F | 6–8 hrs |
| Bananas | Peel, cut in 3/8-inch slices | 135°F | 8–10 hrs |
| Beet chips | Peel, cut in ⅛-inch slices | 135°F | 7–8 hrs |
| Eggplant | Peel, cut in ¼-inch slices, blanch | 135°F | 6–8 hrs |
| Fresh herbs | Rinse, pat dry, remove stems | 135°F | 4–6 hrs |
| Ginger root | Cut in 3/8-inch slices | 135°F | 6 hrs |
| Mangoes | Peel, cut in 3/8-inch slices, remove pits | 135°F | 6–8 hrs |
| Mushrooms | Clean with soft brush (do not wash) | 135°F | 6–8 hrs |
| Pineapple | Peel, cut in 3/8–½-inch slices, core removed | 135°F | 6–8 hrs |
| Strawberries | Cut in half or in ½-inch slices | 135°F | 6–8 hrs |
| Tomatoes | Cut in 3/8-inch slices or grate; steam if planning to rehydrate | 135°F | 6–8 hrs |
| **JERKY – MEAT, POULTRY, FISH** | | | |
| Beef jerky | Cut in ¼-inch slices, marinate overnight | 150°F | 5–7 hrs |
| Chicken jerky | Cut in ¼-inch slices, marinate overnight | 150°F | 5–7 hrs |
| Turkey jerky | Cut in ¼-inch slices, marinate overnight | 150°F | 5–7 hrs |
| Salmon jerky | Cut in ¼-inch slices, marinate overnight | 165°F | 5–8 hrs |

**\*TIP** Most fruits and vegetables take between 6 and 8 hours (at 135°F) to dehydrate; meats take between 5 and 7 hours (at 150°F). The longer you dehydrate your ingredients, the crispier they will be.

# Sous Vide Chart  Crisper Tray not used

| INGREDIENT | AMOUNT | TEMP | COOK TIME |
| --- | --- | --- | --- |
| **BEEF** | | | |
| Boneless ribeye | 2 steaks, 14 oz each, 1–2 inches thick | 125°F Rare | 1–5 hrs |
| Boneless ribeye | 3 steaks, 14 oz each, 1–2 inches thick | 130°F Medium Rare | 1–5 hrs |
| | | 135°F Medium | 1–5 hrs |
| Porterhouse | 2 steaks, 14 oz each, 1–2 inches thick | 145°F Medium Well | 1–5 hrs |
| Filet mignon | 4 steaks, 8 oz each, 1–2 inches thick | 155°F Well Done | 1–5 hrs |
| Flank | 3 steaks, 12 oz each, 1–2 inches thick | 125°F Rare | 2–5 hrs |
| | | 130°F Medium Rare | 2–5 hrs |
| | | 135°F Medium | 2–5 hrs |
| Flat iron | 2 steaks, 10 oz each, 1–2 inches thick | 145°F Medium Well | 2–5 hrs |
| | | 155°F Well Done | 2–5 hrs |
| Beef brisket | 3 lbs, 3–4 inches thick | 145°F | 24–48 hrs |
| **PORK** | | | |
| Boneless pork chops | 5 chops, 6–8 oz each, 2½ inches thick | 145°F | 1–4 hrs |
| Bone-In pork chops | 2 chops, 10–12 oz each, 2½ inches thick | 145°F | 1–4 hrs |
| Tenderloin | 1 tenderloin, 1–1½ lbs, 2½ inches thick | 145°F | 1–4 hrs |
| Sausages | 6 sausages, 2–3 oz each | 165°F | 2–5 hrs |
| Boneless pork shoulder | 3 lbs, 3–4 inches thick | 165°F | 12–24 hrs |
| **CHICKEN** | | | |
| Chicken Breast | 6 breasts, 6–8 oz each, 1–2 inches thick | 165°F | 1–3 hrs |
| Boneless Chicken Thighs | 6 thighs, 4–6 oz each, 1–2 inches thick | 165°F | 1–3 hrs |
| Bone-In Chicken Thighs | 4 thighs, 4–6 oz each, 1–2 inches thick | 165°F | 1½–4 hrs |
| Chicken Leg Quarters | 2 quarters, 12–14 oz each, 1–2 inches thick | 165°F | 1½–4 hrs |
| Chicken Wings & Drummettes | 2 lbs | 165°F | 1–3 hrs |
| Half Chicken | 2½–3 lbs | 165°F | 2–3 hrs |
| **SEAFOOD** | | | |
| Whitefish (Cod, Haddock, Pollock) | 2 portions, 6–10 oz each, 1–2 inches thick | 130°F | 1 hr–1½ hrs |
| Salmon | 4 portions, 6–10 oz each, 1–2 inches thick | 130°F | 1 hr–1½ hrs |
| Shrimp | 2 lbs | 130°F | 30 mins–2 hrs |
| **VEGETABLES** | | | |
| Asparagus | 1–2 lbs | 180°F | 30 mins |
| Broccoli | 1–1½ lbs | 180°F | 30 mins |
| Brussels Sprouts | 1–2 lbs | 180°F | 45 mins |
| Carrots | 1–1½ lbs | 180°F | 45 mins |
| Cauliflower | 1–1½ lbs | 180°F | 30 mins |
| Green Beans | 1–1½ lbs | 180°F | 30 mins |
| Squash | 1–1½ lbs | 185°F | 1 hr |
| Sweet Potatoes | 1–1½ lbs | 185°F | 1 hr |
| Potatoes | 1–2 lbs | 190°F | 1 hr |

**\*TIP** Cook time is dependent on the weight as well as the thickness of food, so thicker cuts of meat will require longer cook times. If your ingredients are thicker than 2½ inches, add more time.

# Steam Chart for the Crisper Tray, bottom position

| INGREDIENT | AMOUNT | PREPARATION | LIQUID | COOK TIME |
|---|---|---|---|---|
| **VEGETABLES** | | | | |
| Artichokes | 4 | Whole | 3 cups | 25–42 mins |
| Asparagus | 1 bunch | Whole spears | 1 cup | 7–12 mins |
| Broccoli | 1 crown or 1 bag (12 oz) florets | Cut in florets | ½ cup | 3–8 mins |
| Brussels sprouts | 1 lb | Whole | 1 cup | 10–15 mins |
| Butternut squash | 24 oz | Peeled, cut in 1-inch cubes | 1 cup | 10–15 mins |
| Cabbage | 1 head | Cut in wedges | 1 cup | 10–12 mins |
| Carrots | 1 lb | Peeled, cut in 1-inch pieces | 1½ cups | 10–15 mins |
| Cauliflower | 1 head | Cut in florets | ½ cup | 5–10 mins |
| Corn on the cob | 4 ears | Whole, husks removed | 1 cup | 4–9 mins |
| Green beans | 1 bag (12 oz) | Whole | ½ cup | 5–8 mins |
| Kale | 1 bag (16 oz) | Trimmed | 1 cup | 5–10 mins |
| Potatoes | 1 lb | Peeled, cut in 1-inch pieces | 1½ cups | 12–17 mins |
| Potatoes, new | 1 lb | Whole | 1½ cups | 10–15 mins |
| Potatoes, sweet | 1 lb | Cut in ½-inch cubes | 1 cup | 8–14 mins |
| Spinach | 1 bag (16 oz) | Whole leaves | ½ cup | 3–5 mins |
| Sugar snap peas | 1 lb | Whole pods, trimmed | ½ cup | 5–8 mins |
| Summer Squash | 1 lb | Cut in 1-inch slices | 1 cup | 5–10 mins |
| Zucchini | 1 lb | Cut in 1-inch slices | 1 cup | 5–10 mins |
| **EGGS** | | | | |
| Poached eggs | 4 | In ramekins or silicone cups | 1 cup | 3–6 mins |

# APPENDIX 2: RECIPES INDEX

Made in United States
Troutdale, OR
04/18/2024

19245739R00044